## AS/A-Level

# Religious Studies

## Philosophy of Religion and Ethics

## Sarah K. Tyler

Philip Allan Updates
Market Place
Deddington
Oxfordshire
OX15 0SE

tel: 01869 338652
fax: 01869 337590
e-mail: sales@philipallan.co.uk
www.philipallan.co.uk

© Philip Allan Updates 2001

ISBN  0 86003 772 X

Cover illustration by John Spencer

Printed by Raithby, Lawrence & Co Ltd, Leicester

# Contents

# Introduction

## About this guide

This question and answer guide has been written to provide you with a resource specifically aimed at helping you in your revision of AS and A2 material for the Philosophy and Ethics papers in religious studies. It focuses on the common topics and issues across all the specifications. It is not exhaustive; some topics feature only on one board specification, and the constraints of space may not therefore allow for coverage of these here. However, the principles remain the same for all topics and you can learn how to apply these to the topics that are relevant to you.

There are 15 questions, all of which (except the synoptic question at the end) have two responses: one typically worth a C grade, the other an A grade. They are interspersed with examiner comments (preceded by the icon 🄮), which will help you to identify their particular strengths and weaknesses. You should attempt the questions before looking at the answers and comments so that you can make a genuine comparison of your work with that of other students working at different levels of achievement. As you work through the questions, read the answers and absorb the principles outlined in the examiner comments. You will become increasingly familiar with the best approach to take and find that your own answers will improve with practice.

## The aims of the AS and A2 qualifications

AS qualifications consist of three modules, which may include a coursework unit. Each module examines a specific discipline within religious studies and all specifications allow for a considerable diversity of options. You may be studying Philosophy and/or Ethics in conjunction with Biblical Studies, Church History or World Religions, so this subject is truly multidisciplinary. Furthermore, if you go on to A2 you will be required to demonstrate your awareness of how the different topics interlink and overlap. This may be in the form of a synoptic unit, which is intended to give you the opportunity to *draw together your knowledge and understanding of the connections between different modules from across your full Advanced GCE programme of study'* (Edexcel). An example of a synoptic question is provided at the end of this book. This will guide you in some of the principles involved in writing a good answer that demonstrates your synoptic skills.

AS and A2 specifications in religious studies are designed to encourage you to do the following:
- **Develop an interest in and an enthusiasm for a rigorous study of religion.** Hopefully, your AS and A2 studies will be more than a means to an end for you. If you are interested in and enthusiastic about your academic studies you will do better in the exam, but you will take away from this subject something that I don't think

you can from many others. It has real 'value-added' features, exploring aspects of human life and existence that are of perennial interest to virtually everyone who thinks about the world and our place in it. A rigorous study is one that involves being critical in the best possible sense of the word: analysing and evaluating the views of others and substantiating your own. If you are not prepared to have your own assumptions challenged in a safe and supportive environment, then religious studies is not for you! You may not come away from it with your views changed, but you will have had the opportunity to evaluate them against those of scholars past and present, and those of your teachers and classmates.

- **Treat the subject as an academic discipline by developing knowledge and understanding appropriate to a specialist study of religion.** This should grow out of undertaking a rigorous study of religion. In the bad old days, people thought that RE, or scripture, was a safety net for those who were not very academic and who needed an easy option. Compulsory study of it in the earlier years at school did not always encourage students to see it as a valuable academic discipline to be pursued in the latter stages of their school career. That has all changed. AS and A2 students will be more than aware of the academic rigour required to do well in this subject, namely acquiring knowledge of the contribution of scholars to the subject and an awareness of what enormous diversity there is in the range of views offered. The discipline is dependent on the skills developed in many others: language, history, philosophical debate in its wider context, and literature. No one would study the works of Shakespeare without recognising it as an 'academic discipline', so why should this not also apply to religious literature? Disciplined scholars relate everything to the question, alluding to narrative and text rather than giving blow-by-blow accounts in ways that may or may not be relevant, and their responses are ordered, structured, and lead an argument to its logical conclusion.

- **Use an enquiring, critical and empathetic approach to the study of religion.** Enquiring scholars seek answers to questions of perennial importance, critically examining the arguments before deciding which they believe to be the most convincing or effective, but not rejecting the views of others without recognising that they are of great importance. Religious and ethical views make a difference to the way in which people lead their lives and scholars must therefore understand why they are held, even if they are not in agreement with them. We need to be aware of the historical, social and cultural influences on the way ideas have developed and of how the past leaves a legacy to the future. There are no 'right' conclusions to reach, but you will gain more credit for recognising the impossibility of definitiveness than for attempting to reach a dogmatic and non-empathetic conclusion.

## Assessment objectives

Assessment objectives broadly fall into two categories:
AO1 — Knowledge and understanding
AO2 — Critical argument and justification of a point of view

More than 50% of assessment is concerned with the first objective, but you will not be able to move into the higher-grade bands if you do not demonstrate your ability to fulfil the requirements of AO2. You will show that you have fulfilled the objectives by the acquisition of knowledge and the deployment of skills. Hence, you need to acquire knowledge and understanding of:

- key concepts within the chosen areas of study and how they are expressed in texts, writings and practices
- the contribution of significant people, traditions and movements
- religious language and terminology
- major issues and questions arising
- the relationship between the areas of study and other specified aspects of human experience

You will also need to develop the following skills:

- recalling, selecting and deploying knowledge
- identifying, investigating and analysing questions and issues that arise
- using appropriate and correct language and terminology
- interpreting and evaluating relevant concepts
- communicating, using reasoned argument substantiated by evidence
- making connections between areas of study and other aspects of experience

As you move from AS to A2 you will be expected to demonstrate a wider range and depth of knowledge and understanding and a greater maturity of thought and expression, so the weighting of the objectives shifts as you move to A2. More marks are proportionally credited to AO2 than AO1.

## Trigger words

The use of trigger words in questions enables you to identify the particular skills you are required to deploy. AO1 trigger words invite you to demonstrate your knowledge and understanding, while AO2 trigger words invite you to evaluate that knowledge. Trigger words you might expect to see in questions may include:

**AO1** Describe, examine, identify, outline, select, what, how, illustrate, for what reasons, give an account of, in what ways, analyse, clarify, compare and contrast, differentiate, distinguish between, define, examine, explain.

**AO2** Comment on, consider, how far, to what extent, why, assess, discuss, consider critically, criticise, evaluate, interpret, justify.

You need to be aware of the difference between 'give an account of' and 'consider critically'. To give an account you draw essentially on your knowledge, which you may *then* be required to evaluate through 'considering critically'. Considering critically, or assessing, or commenting on, involves drawing conclusions about the significance and value of what you have learned. There are certain phrases that you may find useful for this: 'This is important because', 'The most significant is...because', 'However', 'On the other hand', 'It is likely that...because', 'Therefore', 'Nevertheless', 'The implications of this are'. As you work, keep asking yourself 'Why is this relevant to my answer?' and 'What are the implications of this view/issue?' Don't go onto automatic pilot, otherwise you will simply narrate facts or, worse, fiction!

## Learning, revision and exam technique

As you prepare for your AS and A2 examinations there are stages that your teacher will directly help you with, and stages that you must be prepared to work on alone. In the end, teachers cannot go into the exam for you. While they can give you information and guide you in the best practice for utilising that information in the exam, you have to make sure you have learned the material and developed an effective examination technique.

### Lessons

It is initially your teacher's responsibility to select the right information for your needs, but you need to take responsibility for the way you receive it and what you do with it after the class is over. So, develop good classroom habits. Ask questions about the material. Questions can help you to clarify what you have just heard, as well as clear up misunderstandings. Ask questions about the implications of the material the teacher is covering and about how it relates to other aspects of the specification. Your classes also give you the opportunity to practise the vital skill of evaluation. You will hear many views expressed which might be quite different from your own. You can — in an empathetic (i.e. non-confrontational) way — evaluate these: 'Am I right in thinking that you believe X to be right because of Y?' Be prepared in turn for your views to be evaluated by others, and to explain why you hold them: 'I think that Z is wrong because if you take Y into consideration, the conclusion cannot be X.'

### Homework tasks

Because you have to write in the examination — indeed, the written word is the only vehicle you will have for assessment — you must use homework tasks as an essential tool for refining your written skills. One of the most useful things you should be doing for homework is practising past questions, as they will enable you to be totally at home with the way your board and specification require you to use the knowledge and under-standing you have gained. Your teacher can explain to you how he or she has marked your work in accordance with the principles laid down by the exam board so you can gain some insight into the way the system works. Every homework exercise is an opportunity to learn the topic you're working on, so don't just stick it in the back of your file when it has been marked!

### Independent learning and consolidation

Even the best teachers are not going to cover absolutely everything in the class time available, although they will use that time to provide you with virtually all you need to do well in the exam. However, it is the time you put in outside the classroom that will be decisive. You may read an article that no one else in your class has seen, watch a television programme, or simply go over your class notes one more time and, in so doing, finally understand a difficult area. There is no doubt that the top grades usually go to candidates who are prepared to do something extra, rather than simply attending classes and doing the work set.

## Revision for the examination

It is never too early to start revising. From the moment the first topic has been completed in class you should be making concise revision notes, learning quotations and making essay plans. If you leave it until the exams are looming you will only have time to get the information into your short-term memory. You will feel far less able to deal with the unexpected or to spend time in the exam ensuring that your written style is the best you can offer on the day. Revision techniques do, and indeed should, vary. Everybody learns and remembers differently, so don't be led into thinking that you should be doing it exactly the same way as everybody else. Experiment with a range of strategies but make sure they are multisensory. Multisensory techniques literally involve using more than one sense. If you *read* your notes you are employing one sense only, but if you also rewrite them, read them out loud by working with another student or record them onto tape to listen to, then you are employing more than one sense. This will help to reinforce the work of the other senses, and your learning is therefore cumulative.

As you prepare for the examination, make sure that you are absolutely certain about key issues such as the day and time of the exam. You may think this is silly, but I have marked an exam paper on which a candidate wrote: 'Sorry about this, but I only just found out my exam was today'. This is not just a failure on the part of the school (if indeed she hadn't been told) but also a failure on her part for not making sure she did know the right day and time. Knowing dates well in advance enables you to make a revision plan, allocating specific tasks to each day as the exam approaches, so that your revision is never random or unplanned.

You must also be sure of what you will be required to do in the exam and how much time you will have in which to do it. This is why you must practise exam questions to time and not just under homework conditions. The best candidate may achieve a disappointing result because he or she didn't work to time, writing one or two long answers but resorting to a plan, notes, or a one-side long offering for the others. If you have an hour and a half to answer two questions, that means 45 minutes per question, not an hour on one and half an hour on the other.

## The examination

Remember, it's not over till the fat lady sings — so you don't have to be fatalistic about the exam. Keep calm, and even if the questions are not the ones you hoped would come up, you can still use the material you have learned to answer relevantly the questions that are there. Do what you are asked and nothing else. Don't panic and leave early, but think. Read what you have written and check it for careless mistakes and misspellings. Ignore what everyone else is doing, even if they leave the room, faint or cry, and don't spend time in pointless postmortems after the exam.

What's done is done at that stage, and you need to have peace of mind to prepare for your next paper.

### Remember

- **You don't have to be a genius.** If you follow the instructions, are conscientious, thorough and communicate with your teacher, you should do well.
- **It's not just down to being bright.** Remember the hare and the tortoise? The hare had natural advantages but did not build on them. The tortoise was naturally slower but he plugged away and eventually got to the winning post ahead of the hare. I have a student who is naturally an exceptionally clever philosopher, but will he write an essay longer than a side and a half? He thinks being clever is *enough,* when persistence is the more reliable tool.
- **People are there to help you.** You need never feel alone in your quest for a good A-level grade. Every single member of staff at your school is on the same side as you, even if it doesn't always feel like it. But there are also other ways of getting help. Look out for revision courses and one-day or residential conferences, and encourage your teacher to attend exam board meetings. Everyone wants you to do well.

## Tips as you approach your exam

### What the examiner is looking for

- relevance
- coherence
- accuracy
- readable and well-presented answers
- evidence that you have taken an AS/A-level course — i.e. academic answers, not general knowledge

### What the examiner is *not* looking for

- undergraduate-level answers
- perfection
- everything you know, whether or not it is directly relevant
- more than is realistic to expect of a sixth-form student

### How you should approach the exam

- with confidence
- trusting your teacher
- knowing that you have done everything you can do
- knowing what to expect on the paper
- having had lots of practice

### How you should approach revision

- simply
- in your own words
- by getting rid of unnecessary material

- with a pen in your hand
- actively
- in a multisensory manner

**Revision killers**
- reading through your file with music or the television on in the background
- working without a schedule
- working without reference to past questions

### Acknowledgements

It would have been impossible to write this book without the inspiration of my own students, and this one — again — is for Jacqueline, Oli, Melissa, Harrison, Jock, Ed, Gayatri and James (MPW 2000–01). Thanks to you and to all the students who have crossed my path at MPW over the years; what pleasure you have brought to me!

*Sarah K. Tyler*

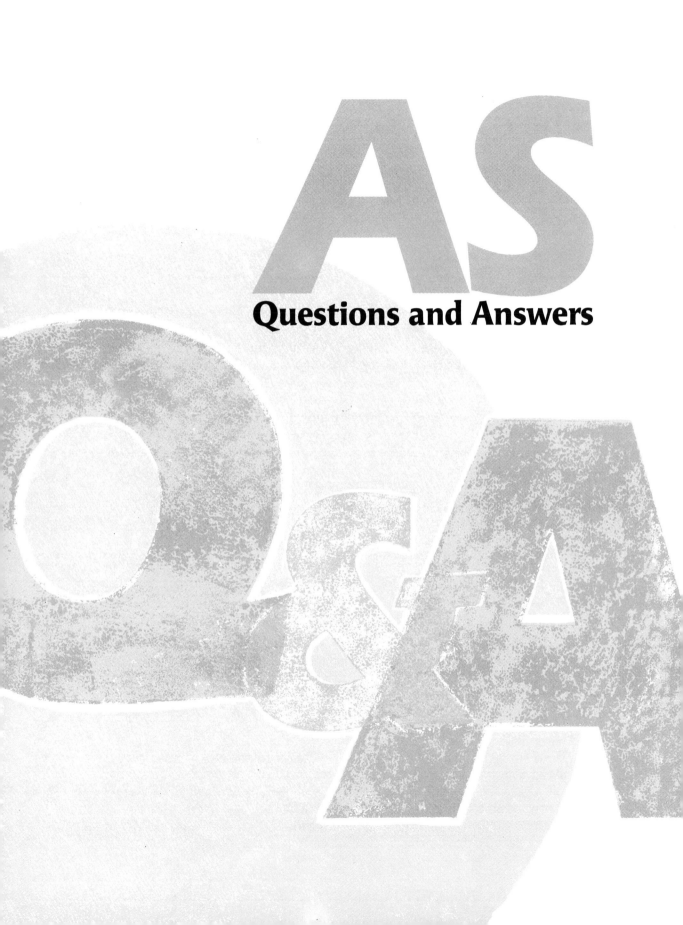

# Questions and Answers

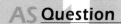

# The cosmological argument

**(a)** Examine the key features of the cosmological argument for the existence of God. (10 marks)

**(b)** For what reasons have some thinkers rejected the cosmological argument? How far is it possible to regard the cosmological argument as strong? (10 marks)

## A-grade answer to AS question 1

**(a)** The cosmological argument is one of the oldest arguments for the existence of God, having been adapted according to theistic principles by Thomas Aquinas in his Five Ways. The concept of a first mover or primary cause had already been identified by the ancients, who had observed that where there is an effect there needs to be a cause, but it was Aquinas who attributed the role of first cause to the God of classical theism. As an *a posteriori* argument, it takes its first principles from an observation of the world. Its premises are drawn from experience, not from analytic truths, and reach an inductive conclusion, that is, one which may possibly be correct, but is not logically necessary. The basic form of the theistic cosmological argument may then look something like this:

P1: All events require a cause.
P2: The universe is an event.
Conclusion: God is the first cause of the universe.

If we accept the two premises, then it may be that we will consider the conclusion to be at least probable, if we have good reasons to think that God is a likely, or even the most likely, cause of its existence.

> **e** We are immediately convinced that this is a good candidate. The essay has not fallen into the trap of simply narrating the details of the cosmological argument, whether offered by Aquinas or anyone else, but rather has identified at the beginning the philosophical principles that underlie the key features of the cosmological argument. Students need to demonstrate their knowledge and understanding of these before they can convince the examiner that they really have appreciated what constitute 'key features'.

The argument is therefore concerned with finding an explanation for the existence of the phenomenon that we call the universe, and rests on the presumption that it is not self-explanatory, but needs to be explained by something outside itself. This is because the argument recognises the contingency of the universe. A contingent item is one which depends on something else for its existence, which comes in and goes out of existence, and which is therefore not self-causing. If the universe cannot provide its own reason for existing then it must have been caused by something else, and that by something else again. Only when we arrive at a self-causing, necessary being can we say we have reached the end of the chain. God is the end of the chain in the theistic cosmological argument.

🅔 Here the candidate is exploring an essential concept within the argument, that of contingency and necessity. The principle of explanation is vital. If the universe were self-explanatory, there would be no need to postulate a necessary being. The candidate demonstrates an understanding of the essential principles behind the argument and, hence, its key features.

The first three of Aquinas's Five Ways are cosmological arguments from motion, cause and necessity respectively. In the first way, Aquinas observes that 'in the world some things are in motion' and that 'whatever is moved is moved by another'. If an infinite chain of movers were postulated then no first mover would be necessary, but Aquinas rejects that supposition, since an infinite chain with no beginning can have no inter-mediate or final mover in the chain. He sees no solution other than to postulate a first mover upon which all other movers in the chain depend — who, he suggests, 'everyone understands to be God'.

🅔 Only now is the candidate moving on to talk about the substance of Aquinas's Five Ways and demonstrating more than basic knowledge. Quotations from the text of the Five Ways may seem excessive, but see how well they are blended into the flow of the answer. This explains the argument, rather than just reciting its basic form.

The second way, from cause, works on the same principle: all things are caused and since nothing can be its own cause, there must be a first cause, on which all other causes depend. In the same way, too, Aquinas rejects the possibility of an infinite chain of causes since such a chain will have no first cause and hence no subsequent causes. It should be noted that although the first and second ways appear virtually identical, the first is concerned with what Aquinas calls the 'reduction of something from potentiality to actuality' (change) whereas the second identifies 'an order of efficient causes'. In both cases God is at the beginning of the chain.

Aquinas's third way observes that 'we find in nature things that are possible to be and not to be, since they are found to be generated, and to be corrupted, and consequently, it is possible for them to be and not to be'. Such things are contingent and hence demand an ultimate explanation outside of them, which is itself dependent on nothing outside itself. In this way Aquinas demonstrates the necessary existence of God *de re*. The very nature of things demands that he necessarily exists.

🅔 The candidate concludes this part of the answer without reference to other accounts of the cosmological argument. This is quite legitimate. There is no essential reason to include anyone other than Aquinas, as long as knowledge and understanding of the key features of the cosmological argument have been demonstrated. This has certainly been done, and recourse to bring other scholars into the discussion may yet be found in part (b).

**(b)** The principles on which the argument is based provide substantial grounds for criticism. David Hume's classic critique found in *Dialogues Concerning Natural Religion* focuses on notions in Aquinas's argument that he finds inconsistent. The cosmological argument depends on accepting the existence of a necessary being and the principle that nothing causes itself. Hume rejects both. He argues that 'any particle of matter may be conceived to be annihilated, and any form may be conceived to be altered'. If this is the case for all else in the universe, Hume asks, why should it not also be the case for the Deity?. What is it about God that renders it acceptable for him to be a self-explanatory, necessary being, while the universe, which we know only through our own limited experience, does not possess such qualities?

> *e* This answer continues to impress. A direct quotation from Hume takes time to learn, but that is what time outside the classroom is for. Again, the candidate shows convincingly that the principles at work here have been understood. This is much better than just regurgitating words on a page, without proper reference to the question.

Furthermore, even if we accept the need for a first cause or mover, which itself may not be logically necessary since it is only from our own limited experience of things again that we are led to this conclusion, why should it be the God of classical theism? Aquinas could be said to be guilty of making an inductive leap from postulating the need for a first cause to the conclusion that only God fulfils such a role. In principle there is no reason why the first cause should not be something or someone entirely different.

Hume also questions the apparent need to explain the whole chain. He argues, 'Did I show you the particular causes of each individual in a collection of twenty particles of matter, I should think it very unreasonable should you ask me what was the cause of the whole twenty'. In other words, if we have an explanation for each effect in a chain of effects then there is no need to seek an explanation for the whole chain. Bertrand Russell made a similar objection: just because every individual has a mother, it does not mean that all men have one universal mother.

> *e* The candidate demonstrates broad knowledge of scholarship and is able to place it in context.

Russell's objection to the cosmological argument was popularised in his debate with the theist F. C. Copleston. Russell rejected the need to seek an external explanation for the universe, stating that, like many things, it was 'just there'. Certainly, the cosmological argument will not find favour if we consider the universe to be a brute fact that need not be explained or investigated further.

Nevertheless, the argument may still be regarded as strong. Copleston maintained that Russell was guilty of refusing to 'sit down at the chessboard' — not entering into the spirit of the argument in refusing to accept that it was even valid to ask questions about the universe. The argument is strong if we believe such questions to be valid. John Hick proposed that 'the atheistic option that the universe is "just there" is the more economical option' but Richard Swinburne employed the principle of Ockham's Razor to suggest that 'God is simpler than anything we can imagine and gives a simple explanation for the system'.

> A confident candidate is able to move smoothly from criticisms of the argument to a review of its strengths. It is good to include dates occasionally, showing that the chronology of these debates has been grasped.

In 1710 Gottfried Leibniz explained the cosmological argument in the form of the principle of sufficient reason. He maintained that even if the universe had always been in existence it would still require an explanation, or an adequate reason, since we need to establish why there is something rather than nothing. We can never reach such an explanation by travelling infinitely backwards in time. More recently, J. L. Mackie argued that we would not expect a railway train consisting of an infinite number of carriages to proceed anywhere without an engine. God is like an engine, not just another truck, but a being that has the power to move without requiring something else to act upon it.

Ultimately, the argument will remain strong if we consider that it is valid to ask questions about the universe and to reach conclusions about it that are in themselves beyond our direct experience. If we are not puzzled about the fact that there is something rather than nothing, the cosmological argument will be rendered invalid before it even reaches the page. If that question puzzles us, then the principles of the argument remain strong, even if we do not accept the conclusion it reaches — that God is the first cause — as the only acceptable answer.

> A good conclusion, because the candidate has driven the point home without repeating material and without the turgid phrase 'Therefore it can be seen that...' or something of that ilk! Overall, the candidate would obtain an A grade.

■ ■ ■

## C-grade answer to AS question 1

**(a)** The cosmological argument for the existence of God can be found in Aquinas's Five Ways, which are *a posteriori* arguments like the design argument. Aquinas argued that because things in the world move and change and come into being there must be a first mover or a first cause. This is because nothing can move itself or cause itself. Aquinas rejected the possibility of an infinite regress of movers or causes because this would not allow for any subsequent movers in the chain. A first mover is absolutely essential for anything to happen at all! Aquinas drew the conclusion that the first mover and first cause had to be God, the all-powerful being that sets everything else in motion.

His argument was a Christian one although it was based on the Kalam argument, which is an Islamic one.

e It is clear that this candidate knows something about the cosmological argument but this rather pedestrian approach is not going to be as successful as the previous answer. The candidate is offering correct information about the argument but has not demonstrated a more sophisticated understanding of the principles on which the argument rests.

Aquinas's third way is slightly different and it sets out to prove that God must necessarily exist. This means that God's existence is not like that of other things or beings which are contingent. Contingent beings come in and out of existence, they are born and they die and depend on other beings for their existence. If the whole universe were made up of contingent beings then nothing would actually exist, since a necessary being is required to start them off. Therefore, Aquinas argues, there must be a necessary being which brings contingent beings into existence. This again is God.

e Again, this is effectively a summary of the third way — accurate, but not especially insightful.

In every stage of his argument Aquinas rejects the possibility of infinite regress and draws the conclusion that every chain must have a beginning if anything is to happen or to exist at all.

e Short sentences such as these may contain fact, but do not suggest developed analysis.

The cosmological argument was supported by Leibniz, who proposed the principle of sufficient reason, which is that everything needs to have a sufficient reason for being. He used the analogy of the book of the elements of geometry, saying that even if many copies of the book existed, one having been copied from another one, there still needed to be a reason why any of them existed in the first place. The same is the case for the universe.

e Again, a legitimate response to the question. The candidate would have done better, however, to provide some explanation.

Mackie also used an analogy of a series of railway carriages that can go nowhere without an engine. An engine is different from the carriages, which are dependent; the engine is not, since it can move itself.

Thus, the cosmological argument has several key features. It looks at the universe and asks questions about how it came into existence because it cannot be explained simply by itself. The argument is based on asking why there is something rather than nothing, and Aquinas and other theists claimed that God was the only answer to this question. Finally, it argues that there must be a first cause, because a chain of causes must have a beginning for anything to exist.

This is more promising, but rather than developing the analysis it falls back at the end on a summary of the second way.

**(b)** David Hume is the best-known critic of the cosmological argument. He argued that Aquinas made too many assumptions, such as that there needs to be a first cause and that the first cause has to be God. It is only within our experience that we see things as the product of a cause and there is no reason why this should apply to the universe. The universe might be its own cause, or be like a vegetable. It is enough, Hume suggested, that we can identify the causes of each individual event in a chain and there is no need to look for a cause for the whole chain, which has been arbitrarily linked together.

This is a good example of a candidate who has understood something of the criticisms against the argument but has not expressed them clearly. What does 'like a vegetable' mean? This needs clarifying, as does the point about individual causes being 'arbitrarily linked together'.

It is also the case that there is no reason why the first cause, if there is one, should be God. We can accept the view that there is a first cause without accepting that it is God, since logically it could be anything, even a red turtle or a fluffy rabbit. The only reason that the first cause might be God is because the believer already has it in mind that God is the only being who could possess the qualities required to be that cause.

The candidate has hinted at some very important criticisms, but to gain further credit the problem of the inductive leap and the assumptions that underlie the theistic argument would have to be explained.

Hume rejected Aquinas's view that God is a necessary being since, he claimed, there is nothing that cannot be conceived as not existing. Anything that exists cannot not exist and this includes God.

Bertrand Russell argued that the universe was just a brute fact and that the argument therefore did not hold water, although Copleston said that he was refusing to sit down at the chessboard and play.

Two short paragraphs that once again fail to draw the credit that more developed discussion would yield.

However, the argument is still popular and could be said to be strong. Even though Russell claimed that the universe is just a brute fact, for many people this is not true since they need to ask the question 'why?' about the universe. There is no obvious reason why it should exist unless something has brought it into being, and we need to find an answer as to what brought it into existence. The argument is also based on something that we can all experience — the universe — not just on an idea that only the believer has. If we are interested in questions about existence then the cosmological argument is relevant, even if we don't agree with its conclusions.

The fact that the argument rejects infinite regress is also a strength, since it is illogical to think of an infinite series of causes and effects. If such did exist then we would have to have travelled an infinite length of time to reach the point we are currently at and this is impossible. Hence a beginning of the chain is necessary.

 We are left feeling that this candidate could have easily gained an A grade if all the good ideas in the essay had been followed through. In this rather undeveloped form, however, the essay would only be worth a C grade.

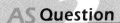

# The teleological/ design argument

**(a)** Examine the design argument for the existence of God. (10 marks)

**(b)** What are the strengths of the design argument? Comment on some of the criticisms raised against this argument. (10 marks)

## A-grade answer to AS question 2

**(a)** The design argument is based on one aspect of the universe — its apparent regularity and purpose. The universe appears to have an end or purpose — a *telos* — towards which everything is working, and for which it has been designed. It may be that this has happened by chance, but the argument is based on the notion that this is less likely than it happening by design, and that therefore a designer must exist who has planned this design and overseen its instigation. Aquinas included a form of this argument in the *Summa Theologica* in the fifth way — 'From the Governance of the World'. He observed that non-rational beings acted so as to obtain the best result, which could not simply be 'fortuitous' but designed.

This is a confident opening that demonstrates knowledge of the argument without out immediately relying on a particular scholar's exposition of it. By the time Aquinas is mentioned we are already sure of the candidate's knowledge and understanding.

The argument relies on an analogy between the works of human design — machines and other artifacts — and the world. The observation that the universe contains features of design is based on the similarities that it seems to share with humanly designed objects and hence leads to the conclusion that just as human machines have a designer, so too must the universe. Like effects presume like causes: human design points to a human designer, and hence the design in the universe points to a designer.

The candidate hasn't missed the important issue of analogy here. This will be particularly relevant in part (b) and suggests an understanding of how it underpins the principle of the argument.

William Paley's analogy of the watch and the watchmaker illustrates this process of reasoning. He used the example of finding a watch on a heath, which could not be satisfactorily explained by saying it had 'always been there'. Its features demonstrate purpose, design and an ultimate function, and all its points unite to fulfil that purpose. Even the materials used are those best suited to fulfil their function, although others

could have been utilised, and even if parts appear to malfunction or if we are ignorant of their purpose, this is not sufficient to disprove that it has been designed.

🅔 Only after outlining the principle of analogy does the candidate refer to Paley. This is far more stylish than automatically summarising Paley's analogy early on in the essay.

Paley was quick to point out that he was not claiming that the universe and the works of human design are exactly the same. Indeed, he observed that the works of nature are greater and far more than those of man, and by implication, the designer of those works is greater than the human designer. God is therefore the supreme designer.

Although the design argument is an old one, it has continued to be popular and F. R. Tennant proposed an aesthetic form of the argument. Beauty is not essential for survival, and yet many things in the universe are beautiful and equipped with far more than they need for simple existence or for the survival of the fittest. Art, music and the deepest human emotions are part of a complex pattern of human experience and suggest a personal, benevolent designer with a real interest in his creation. The God of classical theism would seem to fulfil this description.

Richard Swinburne argued that theism is the best explanation for the design that is apparent in the universe and points not only to the order and purpose that it displays, but also to the providential nature of the universe, which contains everything that is necessary for the survival of humans and animals. This universe is one in which man is designed to occupy the highest position, and the natural laws within it function to make it a place in which man can contribute meaningfully to its development.

🅔 The use of more modern scholarship in its right context is pleasing and it grows naturally out of the earlier discussion of Paley. This candidate demonstrates knowledge and understanding in a very convincing manner.

**(b)** The sceptic David Hume wrote: 'A purpose, an intention, a design, strikes everywhere the most careless, the most stupid thinker.' Indeed, one of the key strengths of the design argument is that even if its conclusions are not universally agreed — that the designer of the universe is the omnipotent God of classical theism — then its essential premises are ones which many recognise as valid, irrespective of religious belief. The beauty of the universe and the way in which it continually amazes and perplexes man gives the argument great appeal, and its premises are easily understood. Poets and hymn writers have used the essentials of the argument in popular forms: 'All things bright and beautiful, all creatures great and small...the Lord God made them all.' So the argument is strong if we believe that the distinctive features of the universe demand an explanation and that the God of classical theism best serves to explain them.

🅔 The candidate has continued to show an understanding of the wide implications of this argument and has referred to the concept of explanation, which is fundamental to these *a posteriori* arguments based on observation of the universe.

Nevertheless, the argument may have suffered a serious blow in Victorian times, when scientific discoveries and the work of Enlightenment scholars revealed that many assumptions that had previously been taken for granted could no longer be so. Fossils in rocks showed that the earth was much older than it had previously been thought, and theories of evolution and natural selection suggested that humans were descended from a less-developed species and could not have been created as the first two chapters of Genesis describe. Many Victorian Christians fell away from their faith following these discoveries, and the principles of design suddenly seemed less to do with a personal deity and more to do with impersonal science.

However, at the same time Archbishop Temple claimed: 'The doctrine of evolution leaves the argument for an intelligent creator and governor of the earth stronger than it was before.' So the design argument could therefore be said to be strengthened by scientific discoveries which show that the universe has evolved over millions of years rather than having existed in the same form for thousands. Scientific explanations could be seen as being compatible with a cosmic explosion, for example, which could be the means that a creator employs, not something that takes place without a creator. Richard Swinburne added: 'The very success of science in showing us how deeply orderly the natural world is provides strong grounds for believing that there is an even deeper cause of that order.' F. R. Tennant also observed that the world is compatible with a single throw of the die and that it seems likely that the die is loaded — the outcome is not the result of chance, but has been determined in advance.

e Intelligent evaluation here, working from a historical perspective and concluding with a modern scholarly view.

Nevertheless, David Hume considered the use of an analogy between human artifacts and the universe to be flawed, since an analogy only works if there are considerable similarities between artifacts. The argument, however, depends on drawing close parallels between the works of man and the works of God, and hence between the nature of the human designer and the divine designer. The danger of anthropomorphism cannot be avoided and if God is compared with human designers then he must share those designers' weaknesses and limitations as well as their strengths. Many human-made machines are designed and built by more than one person working as a team, but proponents of the design argument would not be satisfied with the conclusion that many gods worked together to design the universe. However, Hume maintained that such a conclusion would be inevitable.

e The candidate has successfully raised the criticism that leads from the concept of analogy introduced in the answer to part (a).

Furthermore, there could be many other acceptable explanations for the apparent design of the universe, without making reference to God. The universe is religiously ambiguous, and the conclusion that God designed it is only one of a range of possible conclusions that we might draw from the evidence. Certainly, given the undeniable evidence of evil and suffering in the world, it might be possible to argue that, far from suggesting an all-loving, divine designer, it suggests quite the opposite, since an all-powerful, benevolent creator would not produce a world that was so characterised by evil. The argument, therefore, is strong in so far as it takes evidence from the natural world which may be seen to point to the existence of a designer, but it fails in so far as it does not necessarily suggest that the designer is the God of classical theism.

> e A balanced conclusion, which raises arguments both in favour of and against the success of the argument. Overall, this candidate has demonstrated the necessary knowledge and skills to warrant an A grade. Note too the fluent use of specialist and general written language, which characterises this candidate's work.

■ ■ ■

## C-grade answer to AS question 2

**(a)** In 'The Watch and the Watchmaker', William Paley compares a watch to the world. The watch has features of design which make it unlikely that it has simply 'always been there'. Rather, if we found a watch lying on a heath we would have to come to the conclusion that it had been designed by someone with intelligence and that it was intended to fulfil a purpose. All the parts of the watch work together to fulfil the function that it is designed for.

> e Not wrong, but not particularly sophisticated. It is far better to start your essay with something that conveys your understanding of how the argument works than to plough in straight away with a particular account of it.

Paley argued that this was like the world, and just as the watch could not have come about just by chance, so the world could not be random chance. There are so many things in the world which suggest that it has been designed: birds migrate to warmer climates in the winter, many creatures are perfectly camouflaged to fit their environment, the seasons work in a cycle, and human beings are equipped to be able to survive at many different temperatures. These things may have just come about, but cumulatively they suggest a designer.

> e An example of apparent design is useful, but don't indulge in a list. This cannot gain the candidate many marks.

Paley comes to this conclusion by comparing the world with something that man has made. When people make things, they design them to fulfil a function and choose the parts and the materials which are best for doing that. Paley gives the example of a glass over the front of the watch. Without it the watch would have to be opened on every occasion to see the time (although some watches are designed like that, of course). The metals are those which are least likely to rust. Although Paley chooses a watch as his comparison, any man-made machine would serve the same purpose, as long as it demonstrates evidence of design and function.

e This is all very well, but the candidate has not said anything about the principle of analogy. As we saw in the A-grade candidate's response, this is vital to the argument.

The design argument looks at the world as a whole and identifies many features in it that suggest design. These include the beauty of the world, and the fact that there are many features in it which are not just functional. We could survive without two eyes or ears, but we are better equipped with two. This might suggest a designer whose interest in his creation goes beyond the basic requirements for living, but has a more personal interest in what he is designing. This is good grounds for suggesting that the designer is God. The God of classical theism is a personal, loving God who is involved in his creation from the beginning. He has the power to be the designer, and also the personal commitment to his creation. A world in which there are beautiful things and which provides everything man needs, not only for survival but also for enjoyment, is a world which a loving God would provide for.

e It has taken quite a while to mention God at all in this answer. Only now has it become clear that the design argument aims to prove the existence of God and not just design *per se*.

Finally, even though it may be possible to argue that these things have come about by chance, it would require an enormous coincidence for them to have done so all at once. The astronomer Fred Hoyle said that the chances of the universe producing the basic enzymes of life by random would be around one in ten with 40,000 zeroes after it. In other words, it would be impossible for the universe to have taken the form it has without some kind of design. Believers therefore conclude that the most likely designer is God.

e This is rather interesting. A different scholarly view, which gives the candidate an opportunity for a more thoughtful conclusion.

**(b)** However, the design argument is not without its critics. David Hume rejected it 30 years before Paley had offered his account of the watch, saying that it only succeeded in leading to an anthropomorphic god. Human designs were made by more than one designer working together and so the designer of the universe was far more likely to be more than one god rather than a single god of enormous power and strength.

e No reference to the concept of analogy; not surprising, since it wasn't in (a) either. The candidate offers a relevant criticism, however, and so gains some credit.

Although the universe is very complex and appears to be designed, that does not mean it actually is designed. An argument which sets about proving that the world is designed should come before an argument which tries to prove that the designer is God. After all, not everyone would agree that the universe is designed. There are many features in it which may suggest bad design: earthquakes and flooding, for example, and terminal illnesses. These certainly do not suggest a loving God. Design might just be an illusion.

*Question and Answer Guide* 21

 A number of good ideas all squashed together in one paragraph. The candidate would have scored better if these had been unpacked: there should have been some discussion of the need to prove design in the first place, followed by discussion of the problem of evil *in relation to* the design argument.

Even if the universe is designed, there is no overwhelming reason why this has to be down to God. Scientific discoveries about the universe might suggest that design is caused by a Big Bang or by evolution. God is not the only possible answer. In fact, science could be said to do away with the need for God at all.

 If the candidate had talked about the religious ambiguity of the universe, and the fact that the design argument is inductive and therefore may lead to a number of equally *logically possible* conclusions, more marks would have been scored.

However, the argument may be strong since people do appreciate the features of the world around them, especially beauty in nature, and they wonder at how it has all come to be the way it is. It seems impossible to argue that the beauty of a coral reef and all the multicoloured fish are the work of some random impersonal chance. The world could be much more utilitarian and still survive. Everyone lives in the universe whether they are believers in God or not, and can appreciate it. The argument is based on things that you are aware of even if you don't immediately attribute them to God, like a beautiful sunset, so it could be a good basis for someone coming to have faith in God.

 Strengths at last. The question asks about strengths before criticisms and for a while it seemed as if the candidate was going to ignore this instruction.

There is no reason either why scientific explanations of the universe might not be compatible with the design argument. God might have used the Big Bang as the means of creating the universe and then used evolution as the means of designing it. Christians can be scientists and scientists can be Christians. So the argument may still be strong since an argument which is based on things in the world is accessible to everyone and may lead to the conclusion that God exists, even though it can lead to other conclusions too.

 Unfulfilled potential in this essay means that although there are no glaring errors, it is undeveloped and rather awkward in style. It would therefore be awarded a C grade.

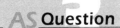
# The problem of evil

**(a)** For what reasons may suffering cause philosophical problems for a religious believer? (10 marks)

**(b)** Outline two solutions to these problems and comment on their success. (10 marks)

## A-grade answer to AS question 3

**(a)** The problem of suffering is an age-old one for believers, and one to which Richard Swinburne claims that the believer must have a satisfactory answer, or there is no reason why the atheist should share his faith. The problem of suffering is 'the rock of atheism' and the biggest single reason why the atheist might consider the theist's faith to be little more than wishful thinking.

> **e** A strong start, since the candidate has opened with a reference to a contemporary scholar and demonstrated understanding of the connections between this topic and another in the philosophy of religion — in this case, atheism.

The essential problem is that if God is omnipotent, omniscient and perfectly good, then why does evil exist in the world? If he is able to remove it, but does not do so, then he is malevolent; if he desires to do so, but cannot, then he is impotent. Neither option surely leaves the theist with a God worthy of worship who fulfils the characteristics of the God of classical theism.

The problem of suffering, or evil, challenges the nature of God and believers must therefore find a way around it if they are to continue to have a meaningful faith. Anthony Flew criticises the inclination of believers to 'qualify' their faith by attempting to adapt the qualities of God to fit in with the problem of evil, and as a consequence ending up with a God who does not fulfil their original definition. When faced with the problem of evil, believers claim that we cannot understand God's reasons for allowing such things to happen, or that we should not measure God's love against human standards. But Flew argues that this effectively means that we change God's nature to fit the circumstances, rather than recognising that there is a genuine problem that needs to be resolved.

> **e** Again, the candidate has avoided aimless citing of different examples of evil and suffering, and shown a more sophisticated awareness of the challenge posed by the problem.

The problem of suffering creates philosophical problems for the believer since conflicting claims must be reconciled: a God who is all-powerful and all-loving, and the existence of evil in the world. The believer will not want to deny the first claim, and cannot realistically deny the other; it is counterintuitive to argue that evil and suffering do not exist when it is empirically real.

The problem of suffering is also a diverse problem since there are so many different types of suffering which the believer must reconcile with the existence of God: moral evil (caused by man), natural evil (presumably outside man's control), metaphysical evil and emotional suffering, animal suffering, and death itself. So the believer needs to reconcile many things if the problem of evil is to be genuinely resolved. The believer must: demonstrate why God has good reasons for allowing evil when he could and should remove it; show that there are good reasons for worshipping a God who chooses not to intervene at all times in cases of suffering; find satisfactory explanations for different types of evil; and consider whether a world without evil would actually be a better one. This will not be possible by just denying the existence of the problem and, as Basil Mitchell observes, believers must 'face the full force of the conflict'.

> Different types of evil have been raised now but still without listing specific events. Rather, the candidate has concentrated on considering the wider problems raised and the need for an explanation if theism is to be meaningful.

**(b)** A genuine solution to the problem of suffering must therefore be one which does not qualify God. All the primary attributes of God must be retained, without denying or ignoring the problem. This kind of solution is called a theodicy. A theodicy does not deny the existence of evil, it does not qualify the nature of God, and it does not suggest that all believers can do when faced with the problem is give up their faith. A theodicy proposes that there are good reasons why God does not intervene when conceivably he could or should do so.

> An informed and coherent introduction to theodicies is more convincing than bowling straight in with a pre-learned summary of Augustine and Ireneaus.

The theodicy of Augustine is based on the Genesis account of Creation and the Fall, and argues that man was created perfectly, but because he had free will (a good thing) he chose to rebel against God and so sin entered the world. All evil and suffering are the consequences of sin. Man's relationship with God and the universe was radically changed and God had foreseen this, but still chose to give man free will since only then could man make a free response to God and be a truly autonomous moral agent. Evil itself is not part of God's creation but is a privation — something which is lacking — as blindness, for example, is a lack of sight. Augustine saw the whole problem in the light of the coming of Jesus, suggesting that God had planned man's redemption through Jesus's death.

> A clear summary which is fresh and yet contains the key elements.

This theodicy places great emphasis on free will, which is its key strength. Free will is a benefit that outweighs all else and it is worth the price of man making wrong choices.

It may be argued that God should have given man free will while ensuring that he never chose wrongly, or that man's wrong choices would have no evil consequences, but this would not be genuine free will and would hence be logically impossible. The other strength of the theodicy is that man's wrong choices are down to him, not to God. God's qualities are therefore protected.

However, the theodicy does depend on an old-fashioned interpretation of Creation and the Fall. Not all believers can accept the literal truth of Genesis and man's creation as a perfect being in the image of God. To blame all suffering on man's first act of sin cannot account for all suffering — animal suffering, for example, or natural evil. The theodicy of Ireneaus might therefore be more successful. He maintained that man was not created perfectly, but only with the potential to grow into the likeness of God. Man has free will to make a range of possible responses when faced with evil, and if he makes the right choice then he will contribute positively to the development of his environment. If he makes the wrong choice then he can retard it. However, since God remains at an epistemic distance from man then these choices are made freely and without God being overwhelmingly obvious to him.

> An evaluation of Augustine's theodicy has blended smoothly into an introduction of Ireneaus's theodicy. This kind of approach generates confidence in the reader that the candidate really does know the subject.

This theodicy allows for all matters of suffering in the world, and sees great value in the opportunity that man has to respond positively. His destiny is not decided on the basis of an event which took place in some primaeval past, but on his own actions and decisions. He is also able to make a real difference to the lives of others, and for this reason Richard Swinburne finds this a useful theodicy, observing that 'a generous God will give us great responsibility for ourselves, each other and the world...(but he) cannot give us these goods without allowing much evil on the way'.

> Ending an essay with a relevant and well-placed scholarly quotation is the hallmark of an A-grade candidate.

■ ■ ■

## C-grade answer to AS question 3

**(a)** The problem of evil is an old one, which can be best expressed by the quotation: 'Either God cannot destroy evil, or he will not. If he cannot, he is not all-powerful and if he will not, he is not all-loving.' Since religious believers believe in a God who is omnipotent and all-loving then they face a real problem, since it is impossible to deny the reality of evil (although Christian Scientists do claim that evil is just an illusion).

> The candidate certainly knows what constitutes the problem of suffering, but has not attributed the quotation to anyone. Although he/she raises the point that we cannot deny the reality of evil, the paragraph has been left rather open-ended.

The problem is an extensive one, since there are many different types of evil which need different explanations. Natural evil, such as earthquakes, volcanoes, illnesses, floods, famine, freak weather conditions such as typhoons and tornadoes, and many other natural disasters, is surely not the kind of feature that a loving God would have included in a world that he created. So the religious believer needs to be able to justify why God does not do anything to remove this evil from the world, or why he would have created such a world in the first place. Moral evil is the evil that man performs and it needs to be explained in another way. If man is capable of performing evil actions then is this the best choice that God could have made? The effect that man's actions have on other people is enormous and man cannot guarantee that he will always be good, even if he does not set about deliberately to do evil and cause suffering. Moral evil includes evils such as murder, rape, torture, cruelty, and other actions which human beings commit against one another. A typical example of moral evil is the bombing of Hiroshima or the extermination of 6 million Jews in the concentration camps. The war in Kosovo is a more recent example.

> A long paragraph with some real potential, but these endless examples of types of evil are pointless. There is only so much credit that can be given for this basic kind of information. The key point is that a world containing these evils needs to be reconciled with the existence of the God of classical theism, and this has been swamped by all the examples.

One way round the problem would be to say that God is not all-powerful, as the process theologians argue. If God works within the universe, trying to bring about the best outcome, but not always able to succeed, then he may still be all-loving, and the fact that he cannot guarantee the best result means that there will be suffering in the universe. However, this is not really satisfactory to religious believers who will argue that a God who cannot bring about the best result if he chooses to (although he may sometimes choose not to) is not a God who deserves to be worshipped and respected. Believers too will not accept that God is not all-loving, since they put their trust in a God whom they believe will always act in their best interests and out of love for mankind. The problem therefore is not easily solved and religious believers have to find a way to reconcile the problem of suffering with the existence of God if they are to continue to believe.

> A more developed discussion of process theology would have been helpful here.

**(b)** The two traditional solutions to the problem of suffering are the theodicies of Augustine and Ireneaus. Both are concerned with showing that man has free will and that it is better for him to have this rather than to be coerced into actions even if they are good. God could have created man without free will and then everything he did would be guaranteed to be good, but if this were the case, then man would not be truly free. True freedom means freedom to be able to make any choice, even a wrong one, and a wrong, but free, choice is better than a right choice not made freely.

**e** It is right to identify and expose the issue of free will here, but the candidate has not really got to grips with it. *Why* is free will better than coerced right choices? Is a coerced right choice a contradiction in terms?

Augustine believed that man was created perfectly and placed in the Garden of Eden, where he fell from grace. When Adam and Eve used their free will and ate from the tree, evil came into the world and we are still suffering its effects now. The world is a fallen world and all we can do is try to use our free will to make the right decisions rather than the wrong ones. The solution will only be found by those who believe in Jesus, Augustine argued, and because salvation through Jesus is a good thing, he called the Fall in the Garden a *felix culpa* — a happy fault — because otherwise man would not have been able to be saved by Jesus's death. This is what Christians continue to believe today.

**e** A very simple discussion of this theodicy.

However, many people argue that it is too old-fashioned to believe in the Garden of Eden and that we know that the Genesis stories are not literally true. Therefore, they cannot be a reliable source of information for believers. Augustine believed that the only origin of evil lay in the rebellion against God of his creatures, but if we do not accept that God created man fully formed and able to rebel against him, then the theodicy does not work. However, if man did reject God in the Garden and continues to do so, then believers will argue that the consequences are inevitable.

The other traditional theodicy is that of Ireneaus, who claimed that God did not create a perfect being in Paradise, but that man is capable of growing into the likeness of God rather than being created in his image. In the world man will be faced with many choices and he can choose the good or the bad, but the main point is that he will make a free choice and therefore if he grows more into the likeness of God than not, it is not because God has determined that he will do so. This is a popular approach since it doesn't depend on believing in the Genesis story, but still allows man to have free will. The world in which man lives is one in which he can genuinely make a difference because he can make different choices. This allows God to be all-powerful and all-loving, but accepts that evil happens in a world that is not perfect and that it can be useful in helping men to grow.

**e** A disappointing conclusion to this essay, which fails to draw out all the useful implications of the Irenean theodicy. This fizzles out without the candidate considering modern interpretations of the theodicy or demonstrating an understanding of its key principles. The examiner would therefore be hard pressed to award more than a C grade.

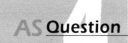

# Miracles

> **(a)** Examine the way in which one philosopher understands the term 'miracle'. (6 marks)
>
> **(b)** Consider the arguments which may be used to discredit belief in miracles and the ways in which belief in miracles might nevertheless still be strong. (14 marks)

## A-grade answer to AS question 4

**(a)** Thomas Aquinas identified three types of miracle under his definition of miracles as 'those things done by divine power apart from the order usually followed in things'. Firstly, he considered those things that God did that nature could not do. This may be considered the most traditional approach to defining a miracle — it is effectively a breach of a law of nature, which contradicts our regular experience about how the world works. Aquinas used the example of the reversal in the course of the sun as such a miracle. We might add walking on water or the raising of the dead as other things which nature cannot do or cause.

> This is an encouragingly substantial discussion of Aquinas's definition of miracles. Even for 6 marks, students should be aiming for something other than a few simple sentences dealing with basic facts.

Secondly, Aquinas identified those acts that God did that nature could do, but not in the same order, for example the recovery from paralysis, or perhaps from a terminal illness. It is not logically impossible for these things to happen, but they are not usually expected. Nature can bring about a spontaneous remission or recovery, but we would not *expect* this to happen and so if it does, it may be attributed to the direct intervention of God.

Finally, he defined as miracles those things done by God that nature could do, but that God did without using the forces of nature. An example of this type of miracle might be recovering from a cold or flu. We would expect this to happen naturally, but if it happened more quickly than usual, perhaps after someone had prayed, then we might call it a miraculous intervention by God.

> The full discussion has continued, fulfilling its initial promise. Each category of miracle has been outlined fully, and in the next paragraph the candidate comes to a rounded conclusion with a brief, but pertinent, evaluation.

Aquinas therefore allowed for a range of possible events that we could call miracles, and did not limit them to violations of a natural law. A miracle, according to Aquinas, is therefore primarily identified by God's intervention. It is an act of God that has beneficial consequences for the recipient and that may include breaking a natural law, but does not necessarily have to do so.

**(b)** One of the key arguments for discrediting miracles is that in fact the definitions of miracle are so broad as to leave them too wide open to interpretation. To say that it is a miracle that someone has recovered from a cold because the believer maintains that God has acted in some special way cannot be verified as miraculous. Rather, it reflects the way the believer looks at the world, and that he or she sees religious significance in events that other people may consider to be coincidence, or fortuitous, or just something that would have happened irrespective of prayer. R. F. Holland used the famous example of the boy on the railway track who, in the face of certain death as a train approaches, is saved when the train's emergency brakes are applied at exactly the right moment. His mother considers it to be a miracle — a divine intervention — but when the incident is investigated, it transpires that the driver of the train fainted because he was ill. It was just a coincidence that it happened at that precise moment. However, the mother continues to maintain that it is a miracle. It is her interpretation of the event that leads her to this definition, and it will make no difference to her how many times she is told that there was a 'natural' explanation for what happened. R. M. Hare would call this a 'blik' — it is her way of looking at the world and nothing can count against this.

> ℮ A long paragraph, but containing plenty of substance. Recognising that this is not a topic best dealt with on the basis of personal opinion or unsubstantiated bias, the candidate has mentioned two scholars — one at length.

David Hume offered a famous argument against belief in miracles, on the basis that people's testimony of miracles is far too unreliable to establish good grounds for believing in their accounts. Firstly, he argued that the probability of miracles occurring is so low that we should be very sceptical about accounts of them. Hume declared that 'a wise man proportions his belief to the evidence', in so far as the evidence for miracles should be considered to be so low as to render belief in them intellectually unsound. Hume was an empiricist, and maintained that sense experience is the only reliable guide to reality. Experience tells us that natural laws hold firm, and since miracles essentially violate such laws then we should exercise extreme caution when evaluating accounts of such happenings.

> ℮ A full discussion of Hume is nicely divided into two paragraphs — one about the issue of probability and one (below) about testimony. This shows a clear understanding of Hume's principles.

Furthermore, Hume argued that accounts of miracles originate from peoples and nations that are themselves unreliable. Miracle stories are appealing to those who love the wonderful and the marvellous — a natural characteristic of mankind in general, Hume maintained, but especially prevalent in religious people. They abound among

'ignorant and barbarous nations', to where their origins can still be traced. In the final analysis, argued Hume, man should weigh the evidence and 'fix his judgement' on the side which is supported by the greater testimony, and in every case he must conclude that natural laws are more likely to hold firm than not.

> **e** Now comes the evaluation, and the candidate has once again used two scholarly approaches to demonstrate two alternative points of view.

However, Richard Swinburne claimed that since people are more likely to tell the truth than to lie (the principle of testimony), we should in general accept what they tell us to be the case (the principle of credulity). In such a case, if someone claims that they have experienced or witnessed a miracle in some way, then we should work on the assumption that they are telling the truth. The biblical writers were aware that the greatest miracle of Christianity (the Resurrection) was so remarkable that many people would not believe it. But religious believers are committed to believing that God can and does intervene miraculously in the world and so, while recognising that such claims are remarkable, they will accept them as an important part of religious belief. Maurice Wiles, on the other hand, suggested that if God performs miracles he should do so more often: a God who will help believers over comparatively trivial incidents but not intervene in the concentration camps is a God whose actions are merely arbitrary and not a God worthy of worship.

Ultimately, believers have to make up their own minds about whether God intervenes miraculously. For atheists it is an incoherent notion, since for them God does not exist. However, there is nothing incoherent in believing that if God exists and possesses the qualities believers attribute to him he does on occasion breach the epistemic distance and intervene in response to the needs of his children.

> **e** The essay ends with a neat conclusion which demonstrates an understanding of philosophical concepts and vocabulary. A well-deserved A grade.

■ ■ ■

## C-grade answer to AS question 4

**(a)** David Hume defined miracles as a violation of a law of nature by 'the volition of the deity or by the interposition of some invisible agent'. There are two main strands to this definition. The first is that miracles breach laws of nature. This is a standard under-standing of miracle and includes miracles such as the parting of the Red Sea, the raising of Lazarus, and the turning of water into wine. These are things that laws of nature forbid and that we know cannot happen without the direct action of God. Hume therefore did not consider other possible definitions of a miracle, such as a beneficial occurrence, or a coincidence that might have religious significance.

> **e** The candidate is quite justified in choosing Hume's definition of a miracle, but could have said a good deal more about his understanding of natural law here.

Secondly, Hume included in his definition of a miracle 'a volition of the Deity or...some invisible agent'. This suggests that Hume did not think that a miracle could only be performed by God, but that some other being might perform it. For a religious believer this would not be acceptable since miracles are only the work of God, and those who perform healings, including Jesus, do so through the power of God and not through any other being or through their own power.

*This is over too soon even for 6 marks. The candidate has not developed a discussion of the philosophical dimensions of Hume's definition and the concluding remarks are really rather thin. Overall, the candidate has not capitalised on a reasonably promising start.*

**(b)** David Hume was an atheist and so he did not believe that miracles could occur. His main argument against them was that religious people are simply not reliable enough witnesses since they have a reason to say that miracles occur even if they do not. Miracles started in uncivilised societies and those who believe them today have not recognised that in a more educated and cultured society they are not accepted as likely to occur. Hume maintained that there are sufficient examples of forged miracles to lead us to be very cautious about accepting the account of a miracle as reliable, especially since religion is founded on miracles and needs to be able to back up their faith claims with them.

*This is all basically solid but the candidate could have included much more detail about Hume's work and evaluated the principles that have been outlined here. For example, why do religious people have reason to say that miracles occur?*

Hume worked on the assumption, however, that religious belief is based on miracles. Although miracles are important to religion, they are not the only things that give credibility to religion. In fact, the Gospels suggest that would-be believers should not base their faith on miracles, but rather that miracles should confirm the faith that they already have. The New Testament does not pretend that miracles are easy to accept either, and Jesus did not encourage people to spread the news of miracles when it was likely that it would lead to misunderstanding. So religious believers are probably rather more cautious about dealing with miracles than Hume suggested.

*All this could be developed further. What is the evidence for the New Testament not pretending 'that miracles are easy to accept'?*

It is often said that miracles do not happen today and this is evidence for them never occurring. However, this is not necessarily the case either. There are many accounts of miracles from Christians today who know that God has worked to answer their prayers, and although there may sometimes be good reason to think that people may be lying or that there may be another explanation, this does not necessarily mean that there always is. Sometimes things may be as people say they are, and if there is no other explanation for why a person suffering a terminal illness recovers then even doctors have been known to say that it is because God has intervened.

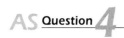

> No scholarship here. These ideas would have been much more convincing if the candidate had been able to back them up with some names and associated ideas.

Religious believers would argue that there are good reasons to support the occurrence of miracles. If God is all-powerful and if he loves men then he is both able and willing to perform miracles. It is a way in which God might encourage believers to go on believing even when times are difficult or when they think that he has forgotten them. On the other hand, it could be said that if God can perform miracles sometimes, then why does he not do so more often? There are many times when people have prayed for a miracle and it has not happened. However, if miracles happened all the time, they would not be miracles, since they are by definition things which do not happen regularly, and we should not assume that God would always answer a prayer with a miracle. If God genuinely loves men, he will act in their best interests, and since he can see the whole picture better than man is able to do, he may know that a miracle is not actually the best thing that he can do. Sometimes people will learn and grow more from suffering or seeing through a difficulty than having it miraculously taken away. A good example of this is Joni Eareckson Tada who was paralysed at 17 years old, but who has said that God used her more through staying paralysed than if she had been healed.

> This is rather interesting, but lacks scholarly depth. The example given at the end of the paragraph has rather a GCSE feel about it. No technical terminology or scholars' views are used.

Lastly, it is the case that sometimes people call a miracle something which is just a coincidence or which can be explained in some other way. If someone passes an exam and says it is a miracle, they don't actually mean that it is a violation of a natural law or even that God had to do something out of the ordinary for them to pass. Therefore, it is easy to discredit accounts of miracles because we can explain them in other ways.

> A typical C-grade response in that nothing the candidate has said is essentially wrong, but it is not substantiated by scholarly contributions or more sophisticated evaluation.

# Morality and religion

**(a)** Outline the reasons why it may be claimed that morality and religion are linked. (10 marks)

**(b)** Examine and comment on the reasons given for suggesting that they are not linked in this way. (10 marks)

## A-grade answer to AS question 5

**(a)** The way in which morality and religious belief may be related is an ancient dilemma going back to Plato's Euthrypo Dilemma: *Are things good because God commands them or does God command that which is good?* That religion and morality are related in some way does seem to be very difficult to argue against, since all religions include some kind of moral teaching and seem to expect their followers to subscribe to some identifiable moral standard. However, why this is the case needs to be examined.

> *e* An encouraging introduction to the essay, which starts to pick up marks from the beginning with a reference to a philosophical principle and the problems it poses.

Firstly, we might argue that religion and morality are related because God is the giver of moral commands and laws. This would support the first question in Plato's dilemma: God makes commands and what he commands is therefore, by definition, good, because God has commanded it. Religious believers might argue that God is the maker of moral commands because he alone has the supreme right and power to do so. He is the creator of all things and nothing can be deemed to be right or moral unless he deems it so. In this way God is the perfect form of the good and all lesser standards of goodness are judged by reference to him. Human goodness is inevitably of a lesser quality than God's goodness, but it still reflects it in some way and makes it possible for man to glimpse what God's goodness is like.

> *e* The candidate has gone on to tease out the implications of Plato's dilemma in an informed and articulate manner.

If we take this position, we need to find how we can access God's moral law. Religious believers are likely to turn to the Bible as the means by which they can establish God's revealed will and find answers to moral dilemmas. The Ten Commandments (Exodus 20:1–17) are arguably the essential guidelines to morality, revealed by God to his people many centuries ago, but flexible enough to be applied to contemporary moral dilemmas. Although they cover only a limited range of moral issues, they are based on intrinsic moral absolutes — e.g. Do not kill — and so they can be applied to questions that are not specifically addressed in the Bible, such as abortion and euthanasia. In the New Testament, Jesus's teaching in the Sermon on the Mount offers flexible and situationist guidelines: 'Whatever you wish that men would do to you, do so to them' (Matthew 7:12). Although Jesus's teaching does not specifically cover all the moral dilemmas that may face modern believers, if they think 'What would I want someone to do to me in this situation?' then they can come to the right conclusion. The 'What Would Jesus Do?' movement, which originated in the USA, suggests a similar process of calculation: in every moral dilemma faced by Christians they should ask themselves what Jesus would do if confronted with this problem and then they will be sure of acting morally.

> ℯ A long paragraph, but plenty of good detail here. The candidate shows an awareness of relevant biblical material and how a modern believer may apply it.

Kant maintained that morality and religion were intrinsically linked, since the moral law demanded that man aim for the *summum bonum*. This is the perfect state of affairs: virtue crowned with happiness. However, because circumstances conspire against man reaching this state in this life, it is impossible for him to accomplish it and it is therefore down to God to bring it about in an afterlife. For Kant, therefore, there could be no morality without God, because without God's agency the moral law cannot be satisfied.

> ℯ Good use of a named, relevant philosopher here.

Finally, if we believe that there are absolute moral commands which perennially hold true, then they must come from somewhere. We may infer them from society and our upbringing, as laws which enable society to live together in harmony, but this makes them impersonal laws. John Wesley suggested that the feelings of guilt we experience when we disobey such laws indicate that there must be a personal agency behind them, and that there is someone to whom we feel responsible and even of whom we may be afraid. In other words, there must be an explanation for the compulsion we feel to obey the moral law, and the best explanation for it is God. If this is the case, then morality and religion are intrinsically linked.

> ℯ The candidate returns to the question in the final paragraph, providing a coherent, well-developed conclusion, but continuing to offer new material right to the end.

**(b)** There are inevitably some problems with this view, however. If God's commands determine that which is moral then, in effect, whatever God commands is morally right, irrespective of what he has commanded. In this case, if someone said that God had commanded them to kill all homosexuals, then technically it would be a moral command, and to carry it out would simply be acting in obedience to God. However, it is obvious that this would not be a morally right action. Simply to say that something is morally right because God has commanded it is therefore not enough, and religious believers must be able to evaluate what they think God is telling them to do. They may think that the Bible supports such a command, as some supporters of apartheid believed that the Bible taught that blacks were inferior to whites, whereas others would say, with considerable justification, that this is a misinterpretation of biblical teaching.

Keeping sight of the dilemma that was considered at the beginning of part (a), the candidate has come back to it effectively for the evaluation in (b). Good use of a modern ethical problem.

This shows how easy it is to justify immoral actions in the name of religion. If morality and religion are linked, then there must be very clear grounds for being able to establish how we determine what God's revealed will is, and what is prejudice or injustice disguised as religion.

The other question that Plato asked in the Euthrypo Dilemma is whether God commands that which is good. If this is the case, then there must be some independently existing standard of goodness to which God is subject. He knows what is good and his commands reflect that standard, but he does not create goodness itself. This is a problem for religious believers since surely they want to maintain that God is above moral standards and beyond goodness, and that he creates it out of his own perfection. If God has to refer to some pre-existing goodness, then his perfection and omnipotence are limited.

🅔 Useful interlinking of material about the nature of the God of classical theism.

Other problems also arise in making the connection between religion and morality. If all religions have a moral code, then surely they will conflict over some issues and who is to say which is right? Christians do not accept polygamy, and yet some other religions, at least in principle, accept it as morally permissible, even desirable. Even within a single religion there can be disagreements. A strict Catholic, for example, might believe that all forms of contraception (except the apparently 'natural' method) are morally wrong, whereas a Christian from a Protestant denomination might consider it morally neutral, or even as a means by which a responsible Christian couple can plan a family sensibly. Some Christians believe that there should be no remarriage after divorce; others that a loving second marriage can be a gift from God. It is therefore very difficult to agree on what is definitively morally right according to religious belief.

🅔 Quite long again, but examples from religious practice are used in a thoughtful way and are related to the question.

The Bible could be said to give very little help, since it was written in a different age altogether and cannot provide relevant and reliable guidance for modern-day believers. It is culturally biased and based on principles that were intended to guide a very different society from the one that has developed today. As a result, it can only give very general guidance and may even be entirely irrelevant. A religious believer, however, may argue that it is not intended to give specific answers to every moral problem encountered by human beings, but that the general principles it offers are enduring. It is up to people to extrapolate from them in order to apply them to their own situations.

🅔 A thoroughly reliable answer, covering a range of useful and relevant material. This definitely deserves an A grade.

## C-grade answer to AS question 5

**(a)** Religion and morality are traditionally linked because so much of religious teaching appears to be about following moral standards and laws. Religious believers will not do certain things for religious reasons, such as have an abortion, support euthanasia, fight in wars, or even work on the Sabbath. Many laws that are followed by non-religious people still have their basis in religious belief. The Ten Commandments include laws that are relevant to everyone, even non-believers — for example, not killing or stealing. Even though religious laws do not govern the UK, in many countries religious teaching is the entire basis for their morality. In an Islamic country, for example, adultery is a crime punishable by death, whereas in this country it is not a crime, although religious believers would generally consider it to be wrong.

> This is worthy and not wrong, but it is all rather general. There is no evidence of the understanding and use of philosophical principles yet.

Religious believers are often expected to follow moral laws more strictly than non-religious people and this could be said to support the view that religion and morality are linked, since a religious believer who acts immorally is often judged more harshly. For people who believe in God, their conscience could be said to be their guide to moral standards. Religious believers might argue that conscience is a God-given mechanism for them to judge whether what they are doing is morally right or not, and if they go against their conscience, the feelings which they have — guilt or shame, for example — are the means God uses to tell them that they are going against what he has commanded.

> The candidate had prepared the ground for a discussion of conscience, which would have been useful and relevant, but has abandoned it very quickly.

The Bible provides considerable guidance for the religious believer, who might say that if they are uncertain of what to do in a particular situation then the Bible will give the answer. It is like God's User's Manual.

> What is this supposed to mean? Such a vague and non-academic statement can hardly be worthy of credit.

We can also argue that religion and morality are linked if all moral commands come from God rather than from society or the legal system. When society agrees that killing is wrong, it is not because the people have come to that conclusion themselves but because they have deduced it as a divine principle. This would suggest that all people are able to know the mind of God, even if they are not outwardly religious. We are continually seeking higher things and recognise that they have value, even if we do not believe in God. In this way God can reveal himself to man through the moral and natural order.

> This is interesting, but again undeveloped. The candidate appears to have learned some relevant points but has not practised developing them in written answers.

**(b)** However, all this can be argued against, since if religion and morality are linked then it creates problems for saying that non-religious people can be moral. If morality comes from God and it is the way he makes himself known to man, then why doesn't everyone believe in God? It might be because they are psychopaths, but there are morally good atheists, who have rational reasons for not believing in God but who are still able to say what appears to be morally right or wrong.

If the Bible is the basis for morality, we have to consider whether it really is a relevant basis. It was written so many years ago that even some religious believers would argue that it cannot be interpreted literally. A commandment such as 'Do not kill' has all kinds of problems linked with it. Does it mean never kill in any situation, or does it mean do not commit cold-blooded murder? If it means never kill, then how can we justify parts in the Old Testament when God tells his people to fight? Islamic belief still includes the idea of *jihad*, a war fought on behalf of God and in defence of religious beliefs, which cannot be right if God commanded no killing under any circumstances.

> 🄔 The same pattern is emerging in this part of the answer. Good ideas are briefly mentioned, but the candidate does not gain full credit for them because they simply have not been expanded.

There are so many areas of conflict between religious believers on moral issues that it is hard to justify the claim that morality and religion are linked. In some churches homosexuality is considered to be such a sin that anyone known to be a homosexual is turned out of the church, whereas others might say that Jesus would not turn away homosexuals and instead they should offer them love and acceptance. If there is such disagreement on moral issues between believers, then how can we be certain that morality and religion are linked? Who could decide anyway? Who are the arbiters of morality?

> 🄔 Rhetorical questions such as these are of limited value unless the candidate attempts to suggest some possible answers.

Therefore, we can see that although religious teaching includes a good deal about morality and what is right and wrong, they are not intrinsically linked since it is possible to learn about morality without religion, and religious beliefs often conflict over what is moral or not.

> 🄔 The candidate would have to have written a much fuller answer to achieve any more than a grade C.

# Utilitarianism

> **(a)** Outline the main features of utilitarianism.                    (10 marks)
>
> **(b)** Examine critically criticisms that have been offered against
> utilitarianism.                                                          (10 marks)

## A-grade answer to AS question 6

**(a)** Utilitarianism is associated primarily with the principle of utility as outlined by the nineteenth-century thinkers Jeremy Bentham and J. S. Mill. The principle of utility defines the sole intrinsic good as happiness or pleasure and the goal of a moral action as the creation of the greatest happiness for the greatest number. Utilitarianism is a tele-ological ethical theory, by which the morality of an action is determined by its conse-quences, and not by the motive for which it is performed. If the consequences are good, then the motivation, even if it is bad, is not brought under judgement. Nina Rosenstand cited the example of a neighbour, charged with watering a friend's plants, who turns on the furnace to warm the house before the friend's return from holiday. The furnace explodes and the house is burned to the ground. Although the neighbour's motivation had been good, the consequences of the action are what matters and, according to a classic utilitarian, the neighbour must expect to be punished for his or her actions.

>  A good, clear understanding of the principles behind utilitarianism has given this essay a firm foundation. As with arguments for the existence of God, it is vital for candidates to demonstrate that they understand the basis on which the theory is founded if they are to be able to evaluate it effectively.

In the form taken by Jeremy Bentham, the quantity of happiness was to be measured so that an individual or, indeed, government could calculate which action was most likely to result in the greater happiness for the greater number. Bentham devised the hedonic calculus, which consisted of seven principles, each of which could be given a numerical score: purity, propinquity, remoteness, certainty, duration, fecundity and intensity. Such a calculation could, in principle, demonstrate who should be saved from a burning house: a pregnant woman, an old man, or a doctor who possessed the cure for cancer. Bentham's form of the principle also considered happinesses to be of equal value; hence, the pleasure derived by the flower-seller in Covent Garden from her weekly bottle of gin was equal to the pleasure derived by the aristocratic couple who attended the opera. In this way, the principle was egalitarian and non-élitist.

>  This is full of good factual material, expressed articulately.

However, J. S. Mill considered Bentham's form of the theory to be 'a philosophy fit for swine', since it valued quantity of happiness above quality. It was possible, according to Bentham's reasoning, to justify the torture of a single prisoner by a group of sadistic prison guards, since their greater number outweighed the pain felt by the one prisoner and the quality of their happiness was not an issue. Mill argued that, instead, quality of happiness was important, and that man should seek the higher pleasures of the mind in preference to the lower pleasures of the body. In his view, therefore, the flower-seller should be educated to enjoy the opera rather than her bottle of gin, and the sadistic prison guards would not be able to justify their pleasure by taking refuge in their greater number. Mill famously claimed, 'It is better to be Socrates dissatisfied than a fool satisfied; better to be a man dissatisfied than a pig satisfied.' The higher quality of pleasure enjoyed by Socrates and the man, respectively, automatically made them more valuable and more morally creditworthy, even if they were, in essence, dissatisfied.

> Examples are given but without the essay descending into tedious narrative. They remain firmly within the context of a critical essay.

Utilitarianism therefore attempts to provide a universal, accessible means for assessing the moral value of an action before it is performed. It makes no reference to precedents, judging every action on its own merits and with no regard for rules or moral absolutes. Even under Mill's formulation, every situation could be considered unique and could be assessed afresh with the interests of the majority in mind. The theory therefore offers a principle on which the majority could enjoy democratic government and society could work in the interest of the masses.

> Some clear evaluation at the end of part (a) sets the candidate up nicely for more critical review in part (b).

**(b)** The teleological principles of utilitarianism are utterly dependent upon the consequences being as calculated and it is this that may be its greatest weakness. The consequences of an action cannot be fully known until it has been carried out, and yet the principle demands that they be calculated in advance, without necessarily taking into account previous situations. However, consequences in advance of an action are hypothetical and cannot be judged with certainty, even if actions of similar kinds in the past *have* produced good outcomes. Furthermore, consequences are far-reaching, and there is no guarantee that any immediate good consequences produced by an action may not be outweighed at some future date by negative ones. The procedure advocated by utilitarianism, therefore, is unrealistic and impractical as a method for calculating the real consequences of an action, only for postulating the possible consequences as far as we are able to make an estimation.

> Once again, we are convinced of the candidate's understanding of the *principles* on which the theory is based.

The principle that the greatest happiness for the greatest number is the sole good to which man should aim is also questionable. Although Mill attempts to distinguish between those happinesses that may be considered to be of lesser value, nevertheless

it still remains a matter of debate whether happiness itself is morally valuable. The theory works on the principle that man will seek the greater happiness for the greater number, even if he himself is not made happy by the action taken. However, even in such a case, the assumption is that the happiness of the majority is the most important goal. Happiness is certainly a good, but whether it is the sole intrinsic good is another matter. What of compassion, love, justice or mercy?

The interests of the majority may in fact permit injustices to be performed. A utilitarian could justify the execution of an innocent person in the interests of keeping the population satisfied, and there is no guarantee that a democratically elected government will not be the cause of great suffering — after all, Hitler's government was elected by the will of the majority. In the same way, while the interests of the majority are being served, those of a legitimate minority are being overlooked, or at least considered to be less important. In its extreme form, utilitarianism may justify the suffering of the minority as long as the majority is happy.

> These are all standard criticisms — nothing especially sophisticated here — but they are expressed coherently and the essay is thoroughly well structured.

Finally, a utilitarian ethic may appear to be akin to that of Jesus in its principles of well-being for others and society, but it makes no reference to divine law or obedience to a divine commander. For the religious believer, God's law overrides the will of the majority, however powerfully demanded, and there can be no compromising the will of God simply to satisfy the masses. The believer is prepared to stand out on a limb and speak up for moral views that may be quite contrary to the popular voice. The will of God is expressed frequently, although not exclusively, in moral absolutes rather than in situationist principles, which may be adapted according to circumstances. The ultimate failing of utilitarianism lies in its rejection of absolutes in favour of a forever-changing morality.

> The candidate has not forgotten that this is a religious studies exam and has introduced some relevant religious evaluation of the theory.

■ ■ ■

## C-grade answer to AS question 6

(a) The ethical theory of utilitarianism judges a moral action as one that brings about the greatest happiness for the greatest number. It is a teleological theory that considers the consequences of an action more important than the reason for it. Jeremy Bentham proposed it as a way of making moral decision-making an easier process and as a principle of democratic government. It relies on being able to calculate the likely consequences of an action and he proposed the hedonic calculus as a method of making this calculation. There were seven principles to consider when deciding on a course of action, including how close the pleasure derived by the action would be, whether it would lead to further pleasure, and whether it would be a pure pleasure or not.

e We get the impression here of a candidate who has learned the basic outline of this theory and who will therefore gain some credit for the information given. But the wider implications of how the theory works, either in practice or principle, have not been grasped.

The theory is one which means that an ethical decision can be made without being concerned about what has been done in previous, similar situations. If one woman has to decide whether or not to have an abortion, she can make the decision which is right for her, and not take into account whether other people think it is right or not, or whether other women facing the same dilemma would have an abortion. Instead she can calculate the possible consequences of her having an abortion in relation to her own circumstances, her family's situation, the amount of happiness she thinks the child might bring to her and whether the child itself would be happy. Under utilitarianism she would not have to consider whether abortion was inherently wrong, but just whether it would be right or wrong for her in her own particular circumstances.

e After the first paragraph, which seems to contain the extent of the candidate's understanding of the theory, he/she is falling back on the old trick of using case studies. There are only so many marks you can get for these and already the candidate is over-burdening the answer with examples.

Vardy used the example of a pregnant woman deciding whether to have an abortion or to go on a skiing holiday. If she keeps the baby she can't go on holiday, but if she has an abortion she can go. A utilitarian would suggest that she calculate as far as she possibly can the consequences of each decision, and it is likely that since the short-term happiness of the holiday would not be as great as the long-term happiness to a wide range of people of going ahead with the pregnancy, that she would abandon the holiday, not the pregnancy. However, if she knew that the baby was going to be born so seriously handicapped that it would have no quality of life then she might decide that holiday or not, the happiness of the child would be so limited that an abortion would be the kindest thing to do anyway.

e More case study material — the point is being laboured without any gain for the candidate.

J. S. Mill was also a utilitarian, but he thought that Bentham was more concerned with lower pleasures than with higher pleasures, which were more intellectual. He rejected the hedonic calculus and said that all men should aim to be like Socrates rather than swine. This was because the theory could justify outcomes that were not truly moral, such as the mother having an abortion simply to go on holiday or prison guards torturing a prisoner because it gave them pleasure. However, the theory does help us to think about the outcome of a decision rather than just acting on the basis of a rule which does not always apply to everyone.

e What does the candidate mean about Socrates and swine? This smacks of half-learned notes without understanding. An abrupt and perfunctory conclusion.

**(b)** The main criticism of utilitarianism is that consequences are not always the best means of judging a moral dilemma. We cannot know all the consequences of an action in advance and can only make a calculation that is based on possible, not definite, outcomes. Therefore any calculation we make cannot be totally reliable and it depends on making very lengthy considerations of possible consequences and even then not being certain that the decision made will be the right one.

> This is basically sound so far, but there is no sign that the candidate is going to discuss in depth the advantages of a deontological theory over a consequentialist one.

In the case of a woman deciding whether to have an abortion or not, she might decide that because there is a good chance her child will be handicapped she will have an abortion in the interests of the greatest happiness of the greatest number. However, it is possible that the child might not be born handicapped after all, or even if it was, there is no reason to suppose that it would definitely be unhappy or bring unhappiness to others. We cannot make a decision on possible outcomes, or at least not a reliable decision. We have to take other things into account as well. If the woman was a Christian, she might believe that even if the child is handicapped, God will give her the strength to deal with it and that it is more important to preserve life and trust in God.

> A relevant but unsophisticated analysis, veering off onto the same old case study again.

The theory, as I said above, can justify immoral actions like the guards torturing the prisoner. One person's happiness is not the same as someone else's, and we should not assume that because more people are made happy by one action rather than another that it makes the action right in itself. Is happiness the right basis for judging the morality of an action anyway? Happiness is sometimes a very superficial emotion and others are of more value to more people. We can be happy because someone we don't like is unhappy, and this is obviously not morally right.

Bentham's form of utilitarianism considers it more important that the majority is happy than that what is actually right is being done, and even Mill's form is flawed because it assumes that everyone wants to pursue higher pleasures. If one person's idea of pleasure is to go to watch football and another's is to sing opera, then why should one be considered better than the other?

> We are left wishing that the candidate had developed all these potentially interesting and relevant points. Another abrupt ending makes this a C-grade essay which, with some refinement, could easily have attained a higher grade.

# Ethical language

**(a)** Explain what scholars mean when they say ethical statements are merely expressions of opinion. (10 marks)

**(b)** How far do you consider such views to be justified? (10 marks)

## A-grade answer to AS question 7

**(a)** Often referred to as the 'Hurray! — Boo!' theory, the emotive theory of ethics grew out of the work of the logical positivists, who sought to do away with all metaphysical language, which they deemed to be beyond empirical verification and therefore meaningless. This did great damage to religious language, since statements such as 'God exists' were considered meaningless, as they dealt with metaphysical concepts. Since metaphysical concepts could not be subject to verification or falsification, then they could not carry any meaning. Therefore even to ask the question 'Does God exist?' was meaningless.

> What a positive start to this essay! Straight to the point and underpinned by a clear understanding of the philosophy of language.

When applied to ethical language, the logical positivists maintained ethical statements were also meaningless as they did not make objectively true claims. The theory of emotivism developed out of this, and its proponents argued that if we make a claim such as 'Abortion is wrong', we are not making a value judgement based on an objective point of reference. Instead, we are simply saying 'I don't like abortion', or more collo-quially, 'Abortion — boo!' On the other hand, if we say 'Abortion is good' it is the equivalent of saying 'Abortion — hurray!' There is no objective content to our statement, which is purely an expression of opinion, and since opinions are not reliable arbiters of moral truth (as Kant had identified), they are meaningless.

> This really is excellent; there is no wasted material and it is all directly applied to the question.

A. J. Ayer (in *Language, Truth and Logic*, 1936) maintained that to say 'Abortion (or murder) is wrong' is nothing more than to make some kind of primitive noise! Ethical claims are not designed to be factual, but to invoke certain emotional responses in the hearer and so what they mean is less important than what they accomplish. They cannot be justified in any rational kind of way, since all we are doing is attempting to encourage other people to agree with our subjective opinions.

> The sign of a confident student here — plenty of well-used, relevant scholarship, illustrating the student's own clear understanding of the principles.

Rudolph Carnap took a similar view, except that he considered ethical claims to be commands, not expressions of emotive opinion, as did Ayer. If we maintain that ethical claims are commands from God then we are effectively taking this line, while providing something of a rational reason for them being commands. Bertrand Russell claimed that moral judgements express a wish, and R. B. Braithwaite maintained that they serve to bind the community together. This is a non-cognitive, or anti-realist, view of language, which takes the stance that language does not make factually true claims, but serves some other function. If we want religious believers to agree to the same opinion, then to express it as a command from God gives it greater power to convince.

C. L. Stevenson argued that ethical judgements express the speakers' attitudes and seek to evoke these in their hearers, but he did allow that our attitudes are based on beliefs which provide reasonable grounds for holding them. We may know that a certain course of action will bring about particular results and thus argue in its favour. Nevertheless, Stevenson did allow that even our most fundamental attitudes may not be rooted in any particular beliefs, in which case they cannot be reasoned about. This makes them rather like Hare's bliks, which are ways of looking at the world that cannot be verified or falsified, because they are simply opinions.

e Virtually a model answer, from a candidate who has learned *and* understood the material and who has practised applying it to the question.

**(b)** However, this approach to ethical language and the claims it makes is far too limiting, as was the approach of logical positivism to language in general. It works on the assumption that ethical statements are judged according to the response of the listener and not on the value of the claims themselves; in other words, that the claims have no objective value. If the claim 'Abortion is wrong' says nothing more than 'Abortion — boo!', then it is not a claim that can be discussed and evaluated and this is, quite clearly, not the case. If nothing more was being expressed than an unverifiable emotive claim, why is the topic of abortion open to such in-depth, scholarly and scientific analysis? The power of the statement 'Abortion is wrong' does not simply lie in how others respond to it — with an equally emotive agreement or disagreement — but in the avenues it opens up for investigation of the claim. If someone maintains that abortion is wrong because they have empirical evidence (say) that the fetus feels pain during the procedure, then they are making a claim that is subject to scientific testing — which has objective, factual value.

e The candidate has written quite a terse response to (b), but it is tight and well focused. There is not always great value in using many words if fewer words can be used effectively and relevantly.

Furthermore, if ethical claims were contingent on emotions then they would change as emotions changed. We feel very differently about things depending on our experiences and our relationships with others, which are themselves changeable. However, irrespective of our feelings, we tend to hold fast to values that we recognise as intrinsic and that set absolute moral standards which apply in any given situation, irrespective of our subjective opinions. Allied to this, if ethical claims simply express subjective, emotive opinions, then they can never be universal claims and there can be no agreed morality on any issue at all. Different speakers would express different opinions and there would be no possibility of meaningful debate between them, since they would be doing nothing more than expressing an opinion with which they may want others to agree, but without the rational foundations for establishing why they should do so.

Ultimately, even if moral statements are carried by the weight of popular opinion, this is not enough reason for acting on them. If the majority of people were of the opinion that euthanasia for anyone over 80 years old was right, it would not make it morally right to carry it out. We recognise that moral views must be, and are, held for reasons that go beyond opinion, and we trust that the whole process of law-making is founded on something more that subjective opinion.

*e* Overall, this candidate has used nothing that is irrelevant, and has remained focused on the question throughout. The result is an answer that gains a well-deserved A grade.

■ ■ ■

## C-grade answer to AS question 7

**(a)** It has been suggested by some scholars that when we make ethical statements we are saying nothing more than our opinions, which are highly subjective. The theory of emotivism argues that when we express an ethical opinion we are aiming to influence others to accept our point of view, so the language we use is language that encourages others to respond emotionally to it. If we say that abortion is wrong, we are saying that we feel that it is wrong, not that it is actually wrong. Our statements are not about making objectively true claims. Not everyone agrees that abortion is wrong, or that slavery was wrong, so it can only be an expression of opinion. If everyone agreed that abortion is wrong then there would be a law that made it illegal in virtually every case and there would not always be pressure groups, religious thinkers and politicians arguing over when it should be allowed, or if it should be allowed at all. Because it is a matter of opinion then there will always be arguments one way or the other.

*e* None of this is wrong, but it is rather repetitive and not particularly sophisticated. There is no mention of any scholars associated with the theory either.

However, if all ethical language does is express opinions, it could be said to have no meaningful content, since opinions are just that — opinions. Our opinions about things might be interesting to us but that does not make them relevant to everyone, and we cannot expect everyone to accept what we say just because we say it. If I say that I think stealing is wrong, then many people might agree, but emotivists would argue that even if many people did agree that stealing is wrong, all they would be saying is the

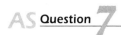

equivalent of 'Not stealing!' in a disapproving tone of voice. This is not a statement of fact but an exclamation like 'Not red shoes with a brown dress!', which is an expression of opinion. We might be hoping that by saying 'Abortion is wrong' we might encourage others to agree with us, but someone else might say 'Abortion is right' and that would be the equivalent of saying 'Abortion — yes!', which is not an assertion. Both people would be offering opinions that are meaningful to them, and which they might hope other people would come to agree with, but they are not objectively true assertions.

> The candidate has understood the topic, it appears, but is not fully explaining the material referred to. As a typical C-grade answer, it promises more than it gives.

This theory is known as the 'Hurray! — Boo!' theory since saying 'Abortion is wrong' is like saying 'Abortion — boo!' This is not a meaningful statement but an exclamation like a primitive noise.

> The answer fizzles out rather suddenly, and there is still no reference to scholars associated with the theory.

**(b)** It is true that the ethical views we express are those that are also opinions and so the emotivist theory of ethics is correct to some extent. But it also assumes that our ethical views are no more than opinions and this is not the case. When people say that they think abortion, euthanasia, killing, stealing or homosexuality (for example) are wrong, they are expressing a view which is usually based on some clear reason in their mind. It is not the same as liking or disliking a colour, or a food, or some piece of music. People's ethical views have significance for them and they affect the way they relate to others and the choices they make.

> These ideas need to be developed, but they have provided some basis for a good argument.

If ethical statements express nothing but opinions then perhaps they may be so biased or subjective that they are meaningless to other people, but they are certainly not meaningless to the person who expresses them. People may have religious reasons for holding their views and they would not therefore think that they were just opinions with no clear objective meaning behind them. If someone believes that abortion is wrong because their religious beliefs lead them to believe that, they will not think that it is just a matter of opinion that is not objectively important. If they believe that God's laws are matters of objective morality (i.e. that they are always right) then they will argue that whether it is their opinion or not is irrelevant. Even if they didn't agree with God's laws, they would still hold true.

> This is potentially quite a complex argument, and it is a shame that the candidate has been so waffly! A tighter style and more in-depth discussion could have developed into something very useful.

Some ethical statements, however, are just matters of opinion. If someone expressed the view that 'Homosexuality is wrong and all homosexuals should be imprisoned', it is likely that some people would consider it a prejudiced point of view and an opinion that they were not likely to share. The person who held it is expressing a view that they may be entitled to express if we have the right to express our opinions, and they may hope that other people will share it. But they must be able to give very good reasons why homosexuals should be imprisoned, since this implies that homosexuality is criminal or at least immoral. While we might agree that taking life is wholly wrong, it is another matter to agree that homosexuality is wholly wrong, since for many people it is natural. So sometimes ethical statements might be expressions of opinion, but at other times they are more concrete than that.

e Still no scholars' names and it really does undermine an otherwise potentially good answer not to include a single philosopher. They should not be the be-all and end-all of an essay, but they are an important way of demonstrating that an academic course of study has been followed. With sufficient development this essay could easily have scored higher than a C grade.

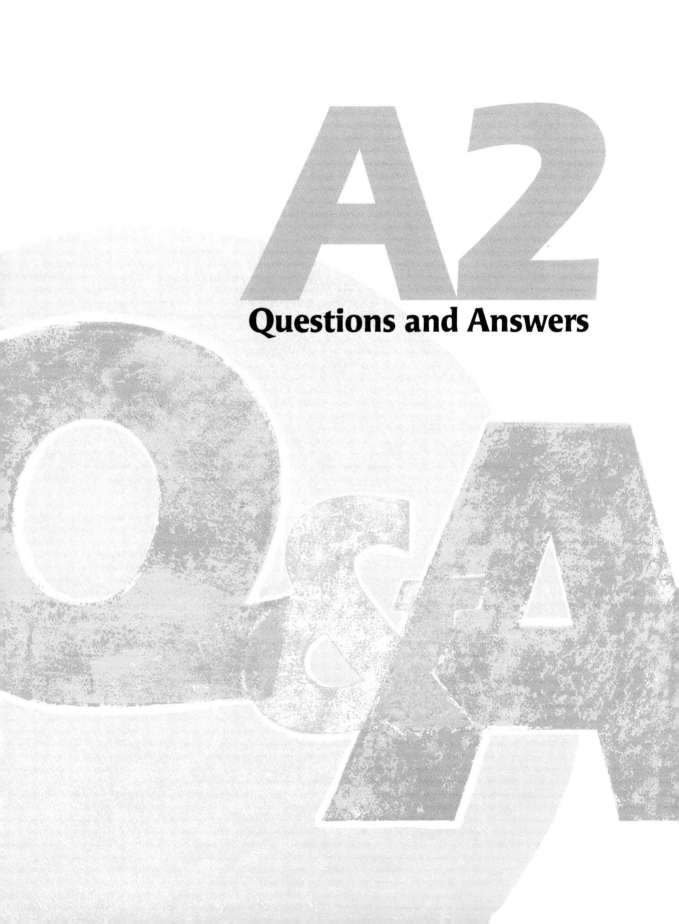

# A2
## Questions and Answers

# The argument from religious experience and the ontological argument

'An analysis of arguments for the existence of God will result in valid philosophical reasons to believe in God.' Discuss and evaluate this claim with reference to both the argument from religious experience and the ontological argument.

(20 marks)

### A-grade answer to A2 question 1

For an argument to provide conclusive philosophical reasons for believing anything it must appeal to reason or to experience. We have conclusive philosophical reasons for believing that grass is green, because experience, guided by the use of the physical senses, provides empirical evidence that this is so — except, of course, when it is dry and brown, and experience and observation tell us that in this case it is not green. Reason and logic tell us that a circle is round since roundness is the essence of circularity, and it is therefore logically necessary that it be so. The rules of mathematics similarly lead to conclusive philosophical reasons for believing that $2 + 2 = 4$. Although some thinkers may well argue that none of these examples need necessarily be the case, it is more likely that most would agree that the philosophical reasons for believing them are generally sound, and accepted as such by even the most sceptical thinker.

e The trick with an essay like this is to make sure that the question is addressed very specifically. Many — if not most — candidates are guilty of simply seeing the words 'religious experience' and 'ontological argument' and setting out to provide the examiner with the sum of human knowledge on the two arguments, without any indication that they have read the question. This candidate has not fallen into that trap and has realised that the question is primarily about the nature of proof.

Can we provide conclusive evidence for the existence of God in the same way? If arguments for his existence are subject to the same principles of reason, empirical proof or mathematics, then we should be able to do so. However, whether they do is clearly open to debate. The nature of the evidence may be considered to be flawed; the premises of the argument may only make the conclusion probable, not logically necessary; the proponents of the argument may not be considered sufficiently objective.

> Only now is the candidate poised to address the two arguments cited in the question, making certain that the wording of the question is kept firmly in view.

The argument from religious experience is an *a posteriori* one. This means that it is based on experience, and if that experience is reliable it may lead to reliable conclusions. However, if the experience is open to interpretation not everyone may reach the same conclusions. The nature of religious experience is highly subjective and so it may, on first viewing, not be considered to be reliable. Since God is metaphysical, it may be considered that even talking about God is meaningless, let alone experiencing him. However, even if we argue that it is meaningful to talk of experiencing God, the debate is not over. Experience of the divine is inevitably subjective, since there are no agreed empirical tests that can confirm whether the best explanation for an apparently religious experience is God rather than anything else.

> Note how the candidate is only using information about the arguments to illustrate the catalyst quotation in the question. Nothing is random; it all serves a purpose.

Philosophers may suggest many valid reasons for arguing that experience of God is essentially unverifiable and therefore cannot provide valid philosophical grounds for believing in his existence. Firstly, the reliability of the experient needs to be taken into account. If they have a history of hysteria, delusion, or if they have strong reasons to seek to justify their religious beliefs, then we need to assess whether the reliability of their testimony may have been affected. Furthermore, religious experience may be the result of learned behaviour, copying others who appear to have had such an experience, or even wish-fulfilment, as Freud explained all religious feelings. It is possible to argue, therefore, that although religious experience, if verified, could be the most successful means for proving the existence of God, it is essentially flawed. Only the experient can say with any assurance that the experience they enjoyed originated in the divine rather than anything else, and even then they may be unduly, or even unconsciously, influenced by factors that lead them simply to infer the divine.

> Remember that the student is not obliged to agree or disagree with the view expressed in the question, but must provide a balanced evaluation.

However, Richard Swinburne argues that unless we have good reasons to think that someone is not telling the truth we should work on the principle that what they say is the case (these are his 'principles of testimony and credulity'). Just because we may not have shared a similar experience, or just because such experiences are unusual, this is not sufficient grounds for doubting the person's testimony.

The ontological argument is an *a priori* argument that is based on reason rather than on experience and is therefore deductive. Such an argument is philosophically valid if it is logically impossible to deny its conclusion, which is based on true premises. It depends therefore on an analytically true definition of God, which Anselm proposed as being 'that than which nothing greater can be conceived'. His argument can be formulated as follows:

P1: God is that than which nothing greater can be conceived.
P2: That than which nothing greater can be conceived contains all perfections.
P3: Existence is a perfection.
Conclusion: God exists.

🅔 Setting out the argument in this way demonstrates the candidate's understanding of how it works as a philosophical proof — the thrust of the question.

According to Anselm's reasoning, the existence of God is analytically true and therefore not simply a matter of faith — he rejoices that even if he were not able to believe in God by faith, he would have to acknowledge that his existence is logically necessary. However, Gaunilo accused Anselm of attempting to define God into existence simply by saying that God is supremely perfect, and a supremely perfect God must therefore exist. By the same logic, Gaunilo argued — *reductio ad absurdum* — you could postulate that there is an island that is supremely perfect and therefore must exist. Anselm worked on the assumption too that the definition of God is without doubt and that it includes existence. While Descartes maintained that existence is as necessary to God as three angles are to a triangle, Kant objected that 'existence' cannot serve as a predicate (a defining characteristic that can be possessed or lacked). Kant therefore did not consider that the ontological argument could provide valid philosophical reasons to believe in God, since it works on a false premise — that existence is to God what circularity is to a circle, or a valley to a mountain.

🅔 The usual scholarly names are included here, but used so that the candidate's knowledge of their contributions is aimed directly at the needs of the question.

The two arguments offer two completely different approaches to proving God's existence and each will work if the grounds on which they are based are not flawed. For the individual who has a religious experience, the existence of God is proved beyond doubt if there is no better explanation for the experience, whereas for others there may well appear to be more likely explanations, drawn on more regular experience. The ontological argument would be foolproof if its premises were analytically true, but even believers may be hard-pressed to accept that God's existence is necessary *de dicto* — simply by definition. Aquinas argued that we must know of God's existence before we can say anything about his attributes whereas, according to Anselm's reasoning, God's existence is one of his attributes, which remains a matter of debate.

🅔 This is an impressive A-grade response. It demonstrates that the candidate understands the demands of the question and has tailored the well-learned information to suit the requirements.

■ ■ ■

## C-grade answer to A2 question 1

The argument from religious experience offers strong grounds for belief in God. For the religious believer, if they have experienced God then no other proof is really needed since he has proved his existence to them in a way that it is impossible to deny. However, religious experiences are flawed in that the person who has had that experience needs to prove to others that they experienced God rather than anything else. A religious experience may be the result of mass hysteria or may be a hallucination. Many religious experiences have been disproved because they can be explained away without reference to God's action. Weeping statues may just be the result of condensation, and a vision may just be the sun playing tricks with the light. The burning bush is a case in point.

@ There are lots of problems here if the candidate is hoping for a high grade. No analysis of the catalyst quotation has been offered at the beginning of the essay, which launches instead into some rather simplistic remarks about religious experience.

The main question about religious experiences is that they are open to interpretation. Everything we experience has to be interpreted and if an experience occurs regularly, or to a number of people, we may believe that we can interpret it reliably. However, when experiences are of things which are beyond regular experience, such as God, or which are not shared by many people, then it is hard to use them as valid proof because the most they might offer is a possibility, not a definite proof. An argument from religious experience is therefore *a posteriori* and all that an *a posteriori* argument can deal with is probability, not proof. Hence, religious experience cannot provide valid philosophical reasons to believe in God.

@ This is rather more encouraging. The candidate has alluded to the wording of the question and there is some evidence that the material is being linked with it. There is not much substance in the answer though, and it is poorly expressed. An examiner would suspect that the topic hadn't been learned very well.

The ontological argument was proposed by St Anselm, a monk, who believed that God was 'that than which nothing greater can be conceived'. He argued that if you have an idea of God in your mind (*in intellectu*) then you must understand that God exists in reality (*in re*). To exist in reality is greater than existing in the mind only, and since God must be the greatest being conceivable then he must exist in the greatest way possible — in reality. Anselm argued that when the atheist said that there was no God he was actually saying what was impossible to say, since if he had understood what God meant then he would have understood that God had necessarily to exist. If this is so then the existence of God was unquestionable since by definition he had to exist.

@ This is not irrelevant, but again the candidate has failed to make this material do anything useful in terms of answering the question. Some marks for basic knowledge of the argument will be picked up, but little else.

This was the main criticism brought up by Anselm's critic, another monk named Gaunilo. He said that Anselm's argument could be applied to anything with the result that it led to absurd conclusions. Gaunilo said that he could imagine a perfect island

and describe all its qualities, but it did not mean that because he said it was perfect it had to exist. In the same way, we could describe a perfect car or a perfect partner, but just being able to describe them does not make them exist. Anselm replied to Gaunilo by saying that his argument was not intended to apply to anything other than God.

🄴 This paragraph, and the one that follows it, are typical examples of those written by candidates who are determined to get the revised material down but do not think out the best way to apply it, and use rather unsophisticated language.

Descartes supported the argument with the idea of a triangle. A triangle necessarily has three sides and three angles and, in the same way, God must have existence. They are qualities that belong to the definition of a thing. Kant rejected this idea, however, saying that although it might not be logical to say that a triangle did not have three sides, it was possible to reject the whole triangle and its angles, and to reject God and existence altogether.

The ontological argument therefore fails to provide a valid philosophical argument for the existence of God because it relies too much on agreeing that existence is a defining quality of God. The argument from religious experience might be more convincing if it was possible to agree that there had been an experience that could only be explained in terms of God and not something else.

🄴 There are elements in this essay that are worthy of credit, but the candidate has lost out in the way the material has been presented. With little direct reference to the question the candidate would be hard-pressed to score a C grade.

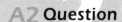

# Life after death

**(a)** Analyse the differences between survival of the disembodied soul and belief in resurrection. (10 marks)

**(b)** Assess which of these two beliefs might provide the stronger philosophical basis for a belief in life after death. (10 marks)

## A-grade answer to A2 question 2

**(a)** A major issue that needs to be considered with regard to life after death is the question of where our identity lies and what part of us needs to survive the death process if we are to enjoy postmortem existence. It is necessary either for our personal identity to survive death unchanged or for us to receive a new mode of being by which we can continue to be real and meaningful once we no longer have existence in time and space. If this is not so, then life after death can have no real significance. However, the two modes of being are quite different in their form and the implications that they have for postmortem existence.

> The question of personal identity is crucial to a discussion of life after death. A good candidate will take time to address this rather than launching straight into a comparison of the two forms of existence.

The traditional Greek view, expressed by Socrates, is that of the disembodied spirit or soul. He maintained that the death of the body can have no real and lasting effect on the soul, which will survive after the demise of the physical body. In *Phaedo*, he wrote: 'Though I have spoken many words in the endeavour to show that when I have drunk the poison I shall leave you and go to the joys of the blessed — these words of mine, with which I was comforting you and myself, have had, as I perceive, no effect upon Crito.' In other words, just because Socrates was confident that after the death of his mortal body he would enjoy another form of disembodied existence, his friends were not so easily comforted. It was hard for them to believe that his body was inconsequential and that he could survive beyond the grave without it.

This view is dualistic: the body is contingent and corruptible whereas the soul is non-contingent and not liable to decay. Descartes conceived of this in his observation 'I think, therefore I am'. Descartes could doubt everything about the physical world but he could not doubt that he was doubting.

> A straightforward response, for which the candidate will gain good credit. It is worthwhile trying to learn as many scholarly quotations as possible, even though it may be hard to absorb ones of the length used in this essay.

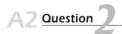 

The Jewish roots of Christianity give rise to the belief in the survival of a resurrected body after death. The body is understood as the total personality which dies and is then raised by the power of God to a new life. This view works on the assumption that the body and soul are not two separate entities as the dualists maintain: 'Man is flesh-animated-by-soul, the whole conceived as a psycho-physical unity' (J. A. T. Robinson). In 1 Corinthians 15, Paul argues for a physical resurrection of a body that is as different from the mortal body as a seed is from the plant to which it gives birth, but which is nevertheless recognisably a body.

John Hick argued for the strength of this position in his illustration of 'John Smith', who disappears from a learned gathering on one side of the world and reappears on the other, without apparently having traversed time and space. He then proposed a similar scenario: John Smith dies in New York but a replica of him appears in London, complete in every way. Hick argued that if we can accept that these strange scenarios are in some way logically possible, then it is also logically possible for John Smith to die and a replica of him to appear in some place inhabited by resurrected beings, and for life after death to be a meaningful concept.

> **e** Once again, the candidate has played a strong card with this use of scholarship. There is no danger that the candidate is going to fall into the trap of offering unsubstantiated opinions.

**(b)** Christians have claimed that there are good reasons for claiming this second model provides a stronger basis for belief in life after death. Aquinas believed that: 'Elements that are by nature destined for union naturally desire to be united with each other; for any being seeks what is suited to it by nature. Since, therefore, the natural condition of the soul is to be united to the body…it has a natural desire for union with the body, hence the will cannot be perfectly at rest until the soul is again joined to a body. When this takes place, man rises from the dead.' Writing to the Corinthians, Paul understood that it was not easy for them to grasp the concept of a new body but he insisted that they do so, describing the resurrection body as the 'perishable' putting on the 'imperishable', the mortal body becoming immortal.

> **e** In this paragraph and the one that follows, the candidate is continuing to build on the secure foundation of scholarly views.

Gilbert Ryle criticised the dualist view as being guilty of making a category mistake. To view the body and soul as being two separate and distinct entities is like watching a game of cricket and asking 'Where's the team spirit?' or looking around all the colleges in Cambridge and asking 'Where's the university?' Such questions fail to recognise that they are part of the whole, not separate entities. Bryan McGee wrote: 'The human body is a single entity, one subject of behaviour and experience with a single history. We are not two entities mysteriously laced together. We have made what Ryle calls a category mistake.'

Although there are weaknesses with John Hick's illustration, particularly the fact that it is something of a stretch of the imagination to envisage the scenarios he suggests, the concept of a replica, created by an omnipotent God who as man's creator can perfectly reproduce him in heaven, is consistent with the view of God presented by classical theism.

A smooth transition from arguments in favour of one view to arguments in favour of the other; this is an essential feature of a well-balanced answer.

Nevertheless, although the body is frequently the means by which we convey mental and emotional states, it is possible to conceive of a mental life that is independent of the body. We are capable of concealing many things and presenting an outward appearance completely at odds with our inner state. We can also transform our outward appearance and yet remain the same person. This may incline us more towards the dualist view of Plato and Descartes. There are practical problems with the idea of the resurrected body which are not inherent in the dualist perspective. Where is this place inhabited by resurrected bodies that Hick proposes? Just because we can conceive of it does not make it a reality (as Gaunilo pointed out to Anselm). Furthermore, if God can create one replica to inhabit this place, why could he not create multiple replicas? In any case, Hick fails to address the fact that a replica is just that — a replica — not the original. Strictly speaking, the same person has not survived the death process, whereas if the body itself were not necessary to establish personal identity, it would not be a problem since personality could survive death intact.

The bodily resurrection of Jesus gives Christians a strong reason for believing that their own postmortem existence will involve the resurrection, or replication, of a body, but despite its pre-Christian associations, belief in a disembodied spirit might prove philosophically more satisfactory.

This very well-crafted answer would receive another A grade.

■ ■ ■

## C-grade answer to A2 question 2

(a) Belief in the survival of a disembodied spirit and belief in resurrection are two different ways of understanding life after death and understanding the relationship between the mind and body. Belief in a disembodied spirit maintains that we are dualistic in nature and that the mind and the body are two separate entities. Plato famously compared the worlds of the seen and the unseen, and believed that the world of the unseen is the world of true reality whereas the world of the seen, which we tend to think of as being the real world, is in fact not true reality. The mind and the body are related in this way. The body is part of the physical world, but because it will be destroyed it is not the real part of a human being but is the vehicle for the soul which, although it cannot be seen, is the real part of man. This view of human nature argues that the body is less important than the soul in which our true personality lies and which is the part of us that can survive death.

> There would be room for some useful discussion of Plato's analogy of the cave here, but this is all rather implicit in the answer.

If we believe that we are more than our bodies, or that our personality is more important than the physical part of us, then we are likely to think that Plato's view (also held by Descartes — I think therefore I am) of the survival of the disembodied soul is attractive. No body would be required in the afterlife and we do not have to consider where the resurrected body might go. Also, survival of a disembodied soul is not burdened with problems about what the body might look like, what age we would be and whether any disabilities we had on earth were still there in the afterlife.

> Use of scholarship is very thin here; brief references to Plato and Descartes just skim the surface of the issues.

Belief in the resurrection of the body is important for those who believe that the body is important as part of who we are and cannot be separated from the soul. This view claims that in an afterlife a body will continue, raised by God in heaven, and although it might be different in some way to the body we have on earth it will be recognisably us. This view is dependent on maintaining that the body and soul must be united as one and are not separate single entities that exist separately from each other. The body needs the soul and the soul needs the body and together they are a total person with a personal identity. John Hick supports this view with the analogy of the man who dies in New York and a replica of him is raised to life elsewhere. An afterlife that involves a new body must in some way involve God making a replica that is exactly like the body we had on earth, though presumably free from the weaknesses of the earthly body.

> This is adequate material (if poorly expressed), but more on Hick's replica theory would convince the reader that the candidate understands exactly what the point is.

**(b)** Philosophically speaking, the resurrected body and the disembodied spirit both have some strengths and some weaknesses. A belief in a resurrected body recognises that the body and the soul are part of one person and cannot be separated. This is supported by the analogy of the man watching a cricket match and seeing all the players, the equipment, the pitch and the umpires, and then asking 'Where's the team spirit?' This assumes that there is something else, something 'other' to the game of cricket that is independent of all the people and equipment and that can be identified separately from them. However, if our body and soul are part of one and the same entity this view will not work. Body and soul serve different functions but could be said to be one entity. Even if we are able to express different emotions with our body from those which we may be feeling in our mind, we are still part of a psychophysical whole and Aquinas argued that an afterlife must include a unity of mind and soul.

> No scholar's name has been associated with the cricket match allusion, and there is no reference to the concept of a category mistake.

There is religious support for the view that mind and body must be united in the resurrection body since in Job 19:25 it says: 'After my skin has been destroyed, then in my flesh shall I see God.' When Jesus appeared to the disciples after his resurrection he was clearly a physical body ('Handle me and see, for a spirit has not flesh and bones as I have' — Luke 24:40), so there is good reason for Christians to support the view of the resurrected body.

> Impressive biblical quotations are used here, but they are no substitute in a philosophy essay for well-used philosophical knowledge.

Philosophically, however, there may be stronger support for a disembodied spirit since it is logically easier to conceive of an existence without the body after death. The body visibly decays on earth after death, so how can it be raised to life? Even if God creates a replica then how can we be sure that it is the same person since a replica is not the original? There can only be one original, as in a painting, and a replica is not as valuable or important. Also, we do see ourselves as being separate from the body and we know that even if we look very different over the years we are essentially the same person, so our body does not limit us. Our personal identity goes beyond it.

> Again, there is plenty of room for the candidate to have developed these rhetorical questions into something rather more substantial. The outline is all here, but this is a typically undeveloped answer that would fail to earn more than a C grade.

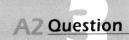

# Religious language: verification and falsification

> **(a)** Explain what is meant by verification and falsification in the context of debates about religious language. (10 marks)
>
> **(b)** Analyse and evaluate the ways in which *either* verification *or* falsification can be used to discredit the meaningfulness of religious language. (10 marks)

## A-grade answer to A2 question 3

**(a)** Meaningful statements are analytic or synthetic. An analytic statement is one that is true by definition (i.e. a circle is round) or tautologous (i.e. all dogs are dogs), or a mathematical statement (2 + 2 = 4). An analytic statement cannot be false, and contains the means of its own verification. Such a statement is a logical proposition and it is necessarily true or false; for example, 'A bachelor is an unmarried man' is necessarily true, whereas 'A spinster is a married woman' is necessarily false. A synthetic statement is verified or falsified by subjecting it to testing. If it can be verified or falsified by use of the senses, it is a meaningful statement. Arguably, if it cannot, it is not meaningful.

> [e] It is important that the candidate demonstrates a clear understanding of the principle of verification before showing how it applies to religious language. This has been done well here.

The verification principle states that only assertions that are in principle verifiable by observation or experience can convey factual information. Assertions that there can be no imaginable way of verifying must either be analytic or meaningless. The logical positivists were concerned to find a distinction between sense and nonsense and the key was that of meaningfulness. Truth and meaning were considered to be distinct concepts, since we can make the statement 'Cows are green' which, although not true, is meaningful because by sense experience we can test it.

> [e] Now the essay is well poised to show how the principle has special implications for religious language.

However, religious language is not open to objective, scientific testing and so religious language statements were deemed meaningless by the logical positivists. Statements about God are neither analytically true nor open to verification by observation, and are therefore rendered meaningless. Even claims to have experienced God are subjective, not universal, and there are no reliable grounds for testing them, hence they cannot be the basis for empirical propositions about God.

Nevertheless, even though religious statements may not be verifiable within this world, they will presumably be eschatologically verifiable, which renders them at least in principle verifiable. Furthermore, Keith Ward observed that God can verify his own existence, and so once again we can argue that statements about God are verifiable in principle, since we know what it would take to verify them.

🄴 The way this question is divided up demands that the candidate be careful about how the material is distributed. This candidate will address the falsification principle in (b), so cannot go into too much detail about it here.

The verification principle was eventually recognised as having serious weaknesses, and the falsification principle presents religious language with a new challenge. In the 1950s Anthony Flew posed the question: 'What would have to occur or to have occurred to constitute for you a disproof of the love of, or the existence of, God?' The falsification principle demands that believers should be able to say what would cause them to withdraw their statements, or to acknowledge that they are seriously challenged if those statements are to have meaningful content: 'In order to say something which may possibly be true, we must say something which may possibly be false' (John Hick). Flew maintained that believers will not allow anything to count against their religious claims and such refusal renders their claims meaningless, since if they are not a denial of something they cannot claim anything either.

**(b)** Flew used Wisdom's Parable of the Gardener to illustrate how believers are guilty of not allowing evidence that fails to prove the existence or love of God actually to count against their theological statements. If a believer is reduced to saying 'God's love for us is incomprehensible' because he or she cannot explain why God is apparently allowing a child to die of an inoperable illness, then Flew maintained the believer is simply allowing their definition of God to 'die the death of a thousand qualifications'.

🄴 The candidate has taken the opportunity to demonstrate a full understanding of the material with well-used quotations from primary sources, but without a blow-by-blow summary of the parable.

Believers must be able to say what would cause them to question and even withdraw their claims about God, even if they are considering it only as a hypothetical possibility. To say 'God exists' must include the possibility that he might not exist or that he might not exist in the way that the believer maintains. Flew argued: 'Now it often seems to people who are not religious as if there was no conceivable event...the occurrence of which would be admitted by sophisticated religious people to be a sufficient reason for conceding..."God does not really love us then."'

🄴 The candidate is demonstrating how straightforward it should be to write a good answer on this topic by following the symposium between Flew, Hare and

Mitchell. The material has been well learned and is represented very capably in the candidate's own words.

R. M. Hare proposed that a believer's statements were 'bliks': ways of regarding the world that are in principle neither verifiable nor falsifiable. Just like the man who thinks all his colleagues want to kill him, and cannot be dissuaded from this despite evidence which is apparently to the contrary, so too believers will not be dissuaded from their belief in God; they will not allow it to be falsified. However, because it makes a significant difference to their lives, the believers' claims are not meaningless. They matter to them and influence the way they interpret the universe and interact with it. Therefore the claims cannot be said to be meaningless.

Basil Mitchell offered the Parable of the Partisan and the Stranger to demonstrate that believers do recognise challenges to faith without allowing them to be conclusively falsified. He described how a partisan meets a stranger during wartime who convinces him that he is on the side of the resistance, although he warns the partisan that his behaviour will not always appear to support his claim. Indeed, the stranger's subsequent behaviour is ambiguous: sometimes he appears to be on the side of the resistance, and on others to be working against it. But the partisan, while realising 'the full force of the conflict' (Mitchell), does not allow it to falsify his belief in the stranger. In the same way, Mitchell claims, believers do not allow anything *conclusively* to falsify their belief in God, but this does not mean it is meaningless because they have recognised that there is a real problem, of which they must be aware.

> ℮ This is quite a long summary of the parable, but it has been contained just in time and it is clear that the candidate understands its application.

Mitchell observed that there are three ways in which believers can react when their assertions are challenged. They can treat them as: 'provisional hypotheses', which they abandon at the first sign of trouble; 'vacuous formulae', which they hold onto without any thought about what might support or count against them; or they can be 'significant articles of faith'. Mitchell argued that since believers' claims about God fall into the third category, they will neither abandon them (the first category) nor, as Flew maintained, qualify them and render them meaningless (the second).

> ℮ This rather abrupt ending is justifiable, since the candidate has said all that needs to be said and avoids a waffly conclusion. This is certainly an A-grade answer.

■ ■ ■

## C-grade answer to A2 question 3

**(a)** The logical positivists were famous for claiming that religious language is meaningless because it does not deal with matters that can be verified or falsified by sense experience. They maintained that only matters of empirical fact or mathematics are meaningful because they can be tested, unless a sentence is analytic when it is self-evidently true.

All other language, they claimed, can be dismissed as meaningless because it cannot be tested or it does not contain some matter which is true by definition.

🔵 No technical language and no scholars' names are used. Basic understanding is here but there is no suggestion at this stage that the candidate is going to be able to move into the higher-grade boundaries.

The logical positivists claimed that religious language statements are meaningless because even the terms used are meaningless terms: God, life after death, miracle, prayer. Such terms cannot be identified within the phenomenal world. To talk about life after death would be to talk about something that is utterly illogical — we are either alive or dead, we cannot be both — and so it is meaningless to use such terms. To make religious claims, therefore, is to make a claim that cannot be verified. 'I believe that I will live after my death' is not a meaningful claim, and even to say 'God exists' is, according to the logical positivists, meaningless. It is not even a question of whether God exists, but rather that it is meaningless to speak of him existing.

🔵 This is interesting, especially the material at the beginning of the paragraph about religious terminology. But the promise is not followed through and the candidate should have had the confidence, and the material available, to develop a fuller discussion. The work of D. Z. Phillips would have proved useful here.

Falsification is concerned with whether religious language claims can be falsified. This means whether anything can count against them. Anthony Flew used the Parable of the Gardener to explain this, claiming that the believer in the gardener was not able to abandon their belief or even question it, when evidence appeared to point against it. This made their claims meaningless, argued Flew. Believers have to be able to say what would make them question claims like 'God loves us', and if they cannot say what would make them question their beliefs then religious language is meaningless. Hare said that religious believers have 'bliks', which cannot be falsified because the believer doesn't really have a good reason for having them in the first place, so they cannot be argued out of them. Mitchell, though, compared the believer to the person who believes that the stranger is on their side even when he doesn't act in support of them.

🔵 All this hovers dangerously on the edge of material only just understood. This may be unfair on the candidate, who may completely understand the subject, but the rather waffly sentences about Hare and Mitchell cannot gain much credit.

**(b)** The verification principle when applied to religious language could be seen to dismiss it completely as meaningless. The verification principle is that for something to be meaningful either it must be verified by empirical testing or it must be an analytic statement. If it does not fall into these categories then it is meaningless. Since religious language did not fall into these categories, it was considered meaningless.

🔵 This all looks fairly promising and includes some technical language that will hope-fully lay foundations for the rest of the answer.

At first glance, this seems to be a very effective way of discrediting religious language. There is always a problem about making religious language statements because they cannot be proved empirically, and often experience actually seems to count against them. How can we prove that God exists in the way that we can prove that a tree exists? We can't. Believers in God have to believe by faith, not because they can test out their claims about God in the way that the scientist can test claims about scientific hypotheses. Claims about God are also not analytic claims since they have to be supported by outside evidence. We cannot simply say that God is loving and it is true in the same way that we might say a circle is round.

e More good material shows that the candidate has understood the principle. Note that this candidate has chosen to concentrate on verification; the previous candidate focused on falsification in this part of the question.

The verification principle was successful in making many types of language apparently meaningless, such as ethical and emotive language. It was very popular at the time and it made philosophers think seriously about how language was used.

e The wider implications of the principle are identified but not sufficiently analysed; this is a rather brief paragraph.

However, it also made other types of language meaningless (not just religious language) and this posed obvious problems. Historical statements such as 'The Battle of Hastings took place in 1066' are technically meaningless because no one can literally verify them. Even scientific statements are unverifiable in their fullest sense — e.g. 'All water boils at 100°C' — because we can't literally test *all* water! Most importantly, the verification principle fails its own test. The principle that 'Every statement should be testable by sense experience or be analytic' cannot fulfil its own criteria of meaningfulness. Therefore, if the verification principle cannot pass its own test, it cannot dismiss other types of language as meaningless if they don't fulfil it either.

e Here is more effective and relevant material, but it is a shame that the candidate has not included any reference to particular scholars.

Religious statements can be verified by other means than those suggested by the logical positivists. Eschatological verification means that at the end we will know whether our religious language statements are meaningful or not. John Hick suggested the example of two people walking down a road. One believes that it leads to the Celestial City, and one thinks it goes nowhere. The person who thinks it leads to the Celestial City interprets what happens on the road differently from the person who thinks there is no particular destination. They interpret things in terms of encouragements or trials. They have similar experiences as they walk along the same road, but it is only when they get to the end of it that one of them will be proved right. It will be eschatologically verified, but while they are walking down the road they simply have to go by faith. This is the case for all beliefs about God. They may not be verifiable in this life, but they are verifiable in principle, so they are not meaningless.

e The use of Hick's parable here is helpful, although it has been told at some length and no evaluation has been given. Overall, this answer has turned into a rather more effective response than part (a) suggested. There is, however, insufficient development of the principles at work, so the candidate does not quite move out of the C-grade range.

WITHDRAWN

# Religious language: symbol and myth

Discuss critically the contribution of symbol and myth to the problem of religious language.

(20 marks)

## A-grade answer to A2 question 4

Cognitive language makes factual assertions that can be proved true or false, for example God exists; God loves us; God will execute a final judgement. When believers make such claims they presumably intend to make assertions that they at least consider to be objectively true. Anthony Flew observed that they are not 'crypto-commands, expressions of wishes, disguised ejaculations, concealed ethics, or anything else but assertions'. Non-cognitive language, on the other hand, makes assertions that are to be interpreted in some other way, as non-literal modes of expression. It is language that serves some other function than expressing factually, objectively true claims. Symbol and myth are two such ways of using language. It is a matter of debate whether religious language is intended to be cognitive or non-cognitive, but if it does deal with matters that are beyond objective, scientific testing then it must include a non-cognitive dimension. If it is entirely cognitive, believers will run into problems when they attempt to verify their claims in a literal way.

The candidate has immediately demonstrated a solid understanding of the fundamental principles of religious language before going on to a discussion of myth and symbol specifically.

A symbol can be described as a pattern or object which points to an invisible metaphysical reality and participates in it (Erika Dinkler-von Schubert). Symbols therefore identify — point to the concept they are conveying — and participate — share in some way in the meaning of that concept. Symbols may be pictorial, abstract, verbal or active (a symbolic action). So, for example, the Cross (a central symbol in the Christian tradition) immediately identifies for believers the death of Jesus, but it does more than simply point to it in a factual way. It participates in it by bringing to the believer's consciousness what Jesus's death signifies, for example salvation from sin, atonement, and God's love for the world.

Clear use of scholarship and relevant examples are evident here.

Paul Tillich used the example of a national flag as a symbol that conveys nationalism, patriotism and national identity. It is more than a sign that simply provides information or instructions, such as a traffic light or street sign. In the same way, religious symbols express what the believer feels about what that symbol conveys. Signs are to do with facts; symbols transcend facts and should therefore not be interpreted literally, which leads only to misunderstanding.

Symbols are therefore subtle modes of communication that belong to higher levels of communication and, while they do not belong exclusively to religious language, they are of particular value to discourse that deals with issues that are beyond the factual and objective, giving them meaning rather than dismissing them as meaningless.

However, although symbols are useful ways to communicate truths that go beyond the factual world, their interpretation can pose difficulties. Symbols can become the focus of worship in themselves and the object of veneration — for example when a believer maintains that it is baptism that conveys salvation, rather than representing salvation that has already been gained. Symbols may be trivialised and their original meaning lost and they can become outdated, like myths. With this in mind, Paul Tillich wrote: 'It is necessary to rediscover the questions to which the Christian symbols are the answers in a way which is understandable to our time.'

e  The candidate has blended positive and negative evaluation of symbol very effectively and the use of scholarship is exemplary.

Myths embody and express claims that cannot be expressed in any other way, frequently making use of symbol, metaphor and imagery in a narrative context. They are not to be thought of as conveying information that is 'not true', but rather as a means of conveying concepts that go beyond basic true – false descriptors to express that which is other-worldly. Mythological language was also used by the biblical writers to speak of eschatological events as well as to describe events that took place before history — Creation, the flood and the tower of Babel are primary examples.

Myths, however, are often criticised as being outdated, and in the 1920s Rudolph Bultmann famously claimed: 'It is impossible to use electric light and the wireless and to avail ourselves of modern medical and surgical discoveries and, at the same time, to believe in the New Testament world of demons and spirits.' He argued that it is necessary to access the kerygma, or the core of religious truth which is concealed by myth, and to do this religious language has to be demythologised. He claimed that myth made it harder for the twentieth-century mind to grasp the truth of the biblical message. However, mythological language is so deeply engrained in religions that it may be impossible to dispense with it altogether, and it is more important to consider how it should be interpreted than to be concerned about trying to establish what 'really happened'.

e  The overall focus is more on symbol than on myth, but what has been included is ideal. In an essay of this type the candidate should aim to divide the time and resources equally, but in this case the quality of understanding and evaluation offset the slight imbalance.

## C-grade answer to A2 question 4

Religious language uses many examples of myth and symbol in communicating ideas about God and religious beliefs. It is fraught with problems because it attempts to communicate matters that are beyond our comprehension and experience. However, we have a limited range of language that we can use because we can only use language that is within our human experience, but which is inadequate to express what believers want to say about God. Therefore, we need to be able to use language that conveys the fact that God is very different from things in the world, and has qualities that are different from human qualities and yet ones which we can comprehend. This is where symbol and myth are useful.

> It is clear that the candidate has a broad understanding of the topic here but, unlike the first candidate, this one does not use technical language and so the effect is distinctly more simplistic.

Symbols are like signs and they can be used pictorially or in words. A typical religious symbol is the Cross for Christians, or for Judaism the Star of David. These are symbols because they say something important about religious belief that goes beyond words. When Christians see the Cross they see something that represents everything about their belief in Jesus and the meaning of his death. It doesn't just represent the *fact* of his death but the *meaning* of it too. Symbols therefore serve to unite believers when they all share the understanding of the symbol, and this sets the believers apart from those who do not know its real meaning.

> Some idea about what meaning is conveyed by the use of these symbols or others would have developed this paragraph.

Symbols can be like metaphors and similes. If we say 'God is my rock and my fortress' we are saying that God shares the qualities we associate with rocks and fortresses. However, we are obviously not saying that he is literally a rock or fortress. This is where symbols are useful but must not be confused with their literal meaning. Symbolic language should serve to make communicating religious ideas more effective but this will not happen if people misinterpret them by taking them literally. For example, when Paul uses the example of a seed to describe the body and how it will be raised from the dead, he does not intend it to be taken literally but it serves to illustrate his teaching about resurrection in a way in which he thinks the Corinthians will understand. Since they were clearly finding it difficult, the use of a symbol is helpful here.

> This is rather fuller and shows a good level of understanding.

Actions can also be symbolic. The Eucharist is an example of a symbolic action that is very important for Christians, as is baptism. Although they may be understood literally — for example that the bread and wine actually are the body and blood of Jesus — more often they are understood symbolically, meaning that they represent Jesus and his death, or the way in which believers have been saved from death.

*e* This paragraph has been left rather hanging in the air.

Myths are stories which may be thought to be untrue, but this is to misunderstand what myth is about. Myths are not just untrue stories; they are stories which are a way of communicating truths that are beyond language. They are not intended to be taken literally, so they can be very helpful in religious language when believers want to communicate ideas that are beyond literal meanings. The Resurrection story, for example, may be problematic if it is understood as a literal story, since there are discrepancies between the different accounts, and it is not clear who Jesus appeared to and in what order. However, if we see it as a myth that contains some important religious teachings then it becomes less important than working out what might actually have happened. The teaching in it might be that Jesus is alive in believers' hearts, or that in some way he was able to live again after death, but how it happened is less important than the fact that believers can live after death too.

*e* This suffers from being utterly without scholarly support. Compare it with the A-grade answer, where the candidate confidently made use of Bultmann's ideas here.

The Old Testament contains many myths that are difficult for modern-day believers to understand and so there are problems interpreting them. It is necessary for believers to decide what their purpose is. If the Creation story is intended to be taken literally, then there are problems for a society which is aware of how scientific discoveries over the last 200 years make it almost impossible to support a literal interpretation. However, myth serves to demonstrate the nature of God and this can be shown in a myth like the Creation story, which is concerned with conveying his power in Creation, and not exactly how he went about creating. When God is described as making man from the dust of the earth, for example, it is intended to show how intimate his relationship is with man.

*e* This is quite substantial, but could have been underpinned by more technical language.

Myth and symbol do enable believers to talk meaningfully about God, but it is important that they are interpreted correctly and that they are used as vehicles for dealing with matters that literal language makes it difficult to convey.

*e* A predictably dull conclusion, which has added nothing more to the essay.

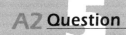

# Atheism and agnosticism

**(a)** Distinguish between agnosticism and atheism.  (5 marks)

**(b)** Analyse one argument for the non-existence of God and consider whether it better supports an agnostic or an atheistic view.  (15 marks)

### A-grade answer to A2 question 5

**(a)** Atheism means literally 'without/no God'. However, there are many reasons why people may hold an atheistic position. Some may hold alternative spiritual views that do not allow room for the God of classical theism, while others may feel that religious belief is irrational and can be explained in terms of other phenomena or social structures. Atheists may never have held a belief in God, or they may have had what seem to them to be good reasons to abandon their belief, possibly because they have suffered experiences that have posed serious challenges to their faith. Whatever their reasons for maintaining that there is no God and that religious faith and practice are therefore empty of any real significance, the atheist has decided that there is apparently no room for doubting the non-existence of God.

> e  The candidate has offered a reasonably full explanation of atheism and has not just written a single sentence defining the term.

The term 'agnosticism' was coined in the nineteenth century by Thomas Huxley. An agnostic may well claim to be open to the possibility of knowledge leading to belief rather than non-belief, but may not be able to say what it would take for them to make that move. Hence, it is possible to say that agnosticism is merely another form of atheism since an agnostic has made no decision in favour of belief in God. An agnostic may maintain that he or she could choose to believe if sufficient evidence were presented to them, although what would constitute sufficient evidence may not be clear.

> e  Similarly, full consideration has been given to the definition of agnosticism. There is certainly a lot more that could be said, but in view of the mark distribution, this is an ideal length.

**(b)** Durkheim's functionalist theory of religion argues that religion plays a function in society: to unite and preserve the community. He defined religion as: 'A unified system of beliefs and practices relative to sacred things...beliefs and practices which unite into one single moral community called a church, all who adhere to them.' He likened a religious community to a primitive clan that worships a totem which symbolises God and the unity of the clan. The clan and God are one and the same. Hence there is no separate entity called God, and thus God does not exist. What does exist is a unified social system that believes it owes its being to God. This belief is expressed in shared rituals, values and identity, and it discourages change.

**e** Along with a well-remembered quotation from Durkheim, the candidate has been very clear in making the link between a critique of religion and an argument for the non-existence of God.

A sociological explanation of religion, which consequently denies the existence of God, was famously offered by Marx, who argued that God was an invention of the human mind in order to satisfy emotional needs. Only by loving one another rather than God can man regain his humanity and reclaim the powers that belong to man but which man has ascribed to God. According to Marx, religion is used by the ruling classes to dominate and oppress their subjects, offering them an illusion of escape. Marx maintained that only when a revolution overthrows the ruling class, and religion is abolished, can the oppressed masses be liberated and recognise their need to rid themselves of religious belief, which is, he claimed, nothing more than 'the opium of the masses'.

**e** Bear in mind that there are two angles to this part of the question, and in order to discuss fully the issue of whether this argument supports agnosticism rather than atheism, the candidate must not get too bogged down in outlining the argument itself.

Any atheistic argument, or critique of religious belief, appears to work on the assumption that while belief in God cannot be conclusively verified, non-belief in God and alternative explanations for religious belief are subject to verification. However, both atheist and theist use the same data and are concerned with the question of the existence of a metaphysical entity. If a metaphysical entity cannot be conclusively verified, surely it cannot be conclusively falsified either, and in principle the atheist's position is no more intellectually sound than that of the theist. A sociological argument attempts to explain religious belief in terms of society and thus to deny the existence of an objectively real deity, but in so doing, Marx and Durkheim simply offer an alternative explanation rather than a conclusive disproof of the existence of God.

**e** This is useful material that shows the candidate has understood exactly what the question is asking for.

In this respect, their arguments must be more supportive of agnosticism than atheism. While it is possible that religious phenomena and the existence of God may be explained in terms of society's functions, such an explanation fails to explain all the features of belief in God. Religious believers distinguish between membership of their religious community and belief in God; their loyalty is to God and not to the community. Yet Durkheim suggests that loyalty to the community is man's primary commitment. His theory cannot therefore explain how religious believers are sometimes prepared to go against society and even to reject it in order to remain faithful to God. Furthermore, society constantly changes, whereas beliefs about the nature of God are timeless and unchanging. Religious believers are often prepared to stand by ideals that appear anachronistic to the non-believer, and yet to the believer are an essential part of their belief in God.

The sociological argument, therefore, may offer a possible explanation for certain religious phenomena. It cannot serve as a conclusive atheistic argument, however, but rather it supports an agnostic perspective that still has room for belief.

> The candidate has provided good criticism of the argument but has not lost sight of the particular angle the question is asking for: agnosticism/atheism.

■ ■ ■

## C-grade answer to A2 question 5

**(a)** An atheist does not believe in the existence of God. They may think that there is no evidence to support belief in God and that those who do believe do so for emotional reasons. An atheist may argue that because there is so much evil in the world, God cannot exist; or someone may have suffered a terrible tragedy that leads them to think that there cannot be a God. An atheist will reject all the traditional teachings about a God who is omnipotent, omniscient and perfectly good, and say that man is in control of his own destiny.

An agnostic will argue that there is not sufficient evidence to believe in God but will allow that if there was more evidence then they might come to believe in God.

> This is a good example of a candidate who has revised selectively. Although the essay begins with a reasonable stab at defining atheism, it is let down by the description of agnosticism, in just the briefest of sentences.

**(b)** For many atheists the main reason why they do not believe in God is because of the problem of evil. Evil is called the 'rock of atheism' because it could be said to provide overwhelming evidence against the existence of the God of classical theism. How can God be all-powerful and all-good if he cannot and will not destroy evil? Atheists argue that even believers should be challenged by the problem of evil, since it is so over-whelming, and if a believer cannot provide good reasons why God allows evil then their belief is not reasonable.

> The problem of evil is a relevant argument to use here, but candidates must be careful not just to turn their answer into a general problem-of-evil essay, repeating material from previous questions answered on an exam paper.

There are two main types of evil — natural and moral evil. Both are given as evidence for the non-existence of God, since he should have been able to control every part of his creation. There is no reason why God should have created a world in which either the natural order brought suffering, like earthquakes and volcanoes, diseases and famine, or in which man performed actions of moral evil against his fellow human beings. God could have created a different world, and the atheist would say that if he chose to create this world in which there are many types of evil then he isn't a God who they would want to worship anyway. It is better to say that he doesn't exist rather than to suggest that he is a God who would allow evil and even create it.

📧 Some reasonable attempt is being made here to link the material to the question.

However, there are many reasons given by believers as to why God does allow evil. The theodicies of Augustine and Ireneaus attempt to suggest that God allowed evil because man had free will and it was not possible to allow a world in which man had free will and yet guarantee that he did not choose to perform evil actions. Augustine claimed that men fell from perfection in the Garden of Eden, but Ireneaus said that man was not perfect in the first place, and so evil is inevitable. However, because man can choose to do the right thing when he is faced with evil, then it is worth having, because the alternative is that the world would be an unreal type of world.

📧 This is all very simplistic — we have yet to be convinced that the candidate is going to produce something above a low C grade.

The problem of evil does support atheism if the existence of God and the existence of evil are incompatible. If the atheist believes that if God exists he should not allow any kind of evil and suffering, or only allow a small amount of it, then the existence of evil and suffering will be sufficient for them to reject belief in God. But it could also be said to be more of an agnostic argument, since there may be good reasons why God permits evil, and the agnostic might argue that they are uncertain of what they are and so they have not committed themselves to belief in God, but if they could be satisfied as to why God allows evil then they might be able to believe in him.

📧 Ultimately, the candidate has answered the question — this final paragraph would not be in a D/E-grade answer — but the essay lacks the sophistication and range to warrant more than a low C grade.

# Natural law

> **(a)** Examine critically what is meant by natural law with reference to morality. (10 marks)
>
> **(b)** Analyse and evaluate the strengths and weaknesses of natural law as an ethical theory. (10 marks)

## A-grade answer to A2 question 6

**(a)** The principle of natural law is that true law is right reason in agreement with nature, which can be applied universally and which is unchanging and everlasting. A proponent of natural law theory will maintain that there is one eternal and unchangeable law valid for all nations and all times, and which is issued by one master and ruler, God. In his *Summa Theologica*, Aquinas argued that there is a moral code towards which human beings naturally incline, and this he called natural law.

> 🄮 Here is a good, clear introduction. There is nothing particularly profound, but it is direct and focuses relevantly and accurately on the question.

Aquinas believed that natural law is accessible through the natural order and that because it is universal, unchanging and relevant to all circumstances it provides the foundation for all moral decision-making and moral knowledge. All human beings can perceive the natural law, because it is available within the natural world, but only believers in God acknowledge that it has implications for them beyond the grave and therefore have a strong sense of why it should be followed.

Natural law draws its inspiration from the Bible as well as from the common reason of mankind. In Romans 1–3, Paul argued that the moral law of God is evident from the nature of man and the world: 'Ever since the creation of the world, his invisible nature, namely his eternal power and deity, has been clearly perceived in the things that have been made' (Romans 1:20). Paul maintained that since natural moral law is so clearly evident in the universe, sinful man has no excuse for wrongdoing. In Matthew 19:3–9 Jesus observed that the divorce law in the Torah was a concession to man's sinful nature and not what God had originally intended in the order of Creation; natural moral knowledge should make it clear that divorce is wrong.

> 🄮 The candidate is building up the substance of the answer here, using the thinking of a known philosopher — Aquinas — and illustrating the answer with well-learned biblical examples.

The principle of natural law depends on establishing the purpose of human life, and Aquinas maintained that that purpose is to live, reproduce, learn, worship God and order society. All things must operate in accordance with these principles to which man is naturally inclined, and God gives man reason to accomplish these purposes whether man believes in him or not. The natural law, instituted by God, gives man the opportunity to work towards the good in all things. Paul recognised, however, that this is not always possible, 'since all have sinned and fallen short of the glory of God' (Romans 3:23). Human beings will fall short of God's best for them because this is a fallen world and they violated the perfect relationship with God and the natural order that was instituted at Creation. Nevertheless, the rational person will desire communication with God and will act to accomplish it, despite the limitations of humanity. Any action that takes humanity closer to this goal is good, and any action that takes it further away is wrong. Aquinas maintained that everybody also has a purpose specific to them, which will fulfil the skills and talents given to them by God. While the goal of a relationship with God is open to all, other goals are only open to some.

> The candidate has clearly and efficiently fulfilled what is required for this answer. It is articulately written, direct and provides substantial evidence of good revision of fully comprehended material.

**(b)** Natural law theory could be said to be strong because it is a simple, universal guide for judging the moral value of human actions, and the purposes that Aquinas proposed for human existence are those that are common to all people. Moral law is made accessible by our reason, and it makes God's reason accessible to a believer because humans and God share the same rationality. Upholders of naturalism would argue that the law ought to reflect the universal set of morals that all people can discern from the universe in this way. It provides a very straightforward set of rules for making moral decisions, claiming that all we need to do is look at the evidence of the natural world and apply our reason, and we will come to the right conclusion. Nature cannot guide us wrongly.

> This is well structured, considering the strengths of the theory first before moving on to the weaknesses. Sometimes candidates are in such a hurry to criticise the argument or theory that insufficient space is given to its strengths.

However, Aquinas assumed that all humans seek to worship God and many would see this as artificial, not natural. If belief in God grows out of psychological or sociological need then it is not natural in the sense that Aquinas intended. The moral reasoning that humans acquire on the basis of that belief serves or reinforces the society in which they live or their own psychological needs. Furthermore, Aquinas gave pride of place to reproduction as one of the common, universal aims of mankind. In so doing he opened up thorny issues for homosexuals and for those who are biologically incapable of having children, let alone those who for personal reasons choose not to do so, such as those who dedicate themselves to celibacy for religious reasons.

> It is always good practice to show the perennial nature of any theological or philosophical debate, and this has been well done here. In the next paragraph a link has been made to the cultural influences on the thinking of Aquinas's own time.

Aquinas thought of every individual and every part of every individual as having a particular function to fulfil. This goes against the 'portfolio' thinking of modern times, by which we recognise the variety of functions that people can fulfil. Rather, it is a concept borrowed from the thinking of ancient Greek philosophy, which maintained that a society in which every individual served a single purpose was an ordered and efficient society. Natural law theory allows no room for situationism, relativism, consequentialism or individualism. It is highly prescriptive and does not allow room for any flexibility.

Finally, Aquinas committed the naturalistic fallacy: he maintained that moral law comes from God (a matter of fact in his thinking) and therefore we ought to obey it (a value judgement). This is an example of the 'is–ought' gap in moral thinking: just because we maintain that something is a matter of fact does not make it a matter of value. Even if moral law comes from God, that does not mean that everyone will agree that we ought to obey it.

*e* The reference to the naturalistic fallacy in this final paragraph demonstrates some clear thinking about philosophical principles in general. Overall, this is a well-deserved A-grade essay that has been written in a very straightforward and direct style.

■ ■ ■

## C-grade answer to A2 question 6

**(a)** Natural law theory is very popular with Catholics. It follows the example of nature, and argues that whatever is natural is right. Therefore, abortion cannot be right because in nature animals do not have abortions (miscarriages are natural though, so this argument applies to therapeutic abortions only).

*e* Oh dear! Not a very encouraging beginning to this essay, with overly generalised statements and a very simplistic response.

It could be a very good way to make moral judgements, however, since it teaches that God has laid down in natural law everything we need to know to be able to solve moral problems. Man can work out from nature what is right because God has also given him the reasoning faculties to be able to do this and he can apply reason to every situation he is in. From this he can derive human laws, but they are ultimately based on God's laws, which are built into the universe and the natural order.

Aquinas was the founder of natural law and he argued that it was a universal principle that was unchanging and would always provide morally right guidance for man. It is a biblical principle and relies on an understanding of biblical teachings such as the Fall. In Genesis, man's creation is described as perfect, but he fell from perfection and a relationship with God. His moral understanding was therefore corrupted and he does not know instinctively what is morally right, although he was created in a relationship with God. However, God has provided man with the ability to know what is right, even if he doesn't believe in him. For those who believe in God it is obviously easier to work out what is morally right than for those who do not.

*Compare this with the work of the A-grade candidate and see how essentially the same material has been used so much more effectively in the earlier answer.*

Natural law theory also maintains that everything has a single purpose, although it doesn't really suggest how we can work out what that purpose is. This is particularly relevant for issues such as contraception. If the only purpose of sex is to procreate then contraception is wrong, but if it has other purposes, then contraception may be not be morally wrong. However, we do need to know how we establish what that purpose is. Even if we say that the Bible is the source of all we need to know about morality, there are problems when we apply it to the present day.

*The candidate is introducing material here that would be better applied to (b) — an evaluation of natural law theory. This inevitably begs the question of what will be done when (b) is reached. Repeated material cannot be credited twice.*

In the same way, Aquinas believed that all human beings have a purpose to fulfil and that they should seek to find what this is. While each person will have a purpose which is particular to them, all humanity has the purpose of seeking communion with God, the purpose for which humanity was created. This again assumes that human beings will both want a relationship with God and be able to find God in some way so that they can establish their purpose and fulfil it. Fulfilling the right purpose in all things is what is 'good' and hence natural law defines good as being that which is natural. That which is unnatural is therefore, by definition, not good.

*The candidate has returned to a broader discussion of what constitutes natural law theory, but has provided a rather limp answer. A good number of marks will need to be picked up in (b) if the essay is to move into the higher-grade boundaries.*

**(b)** Natural law theory is still popular with some religious thinkers but it has its limitations as a workable ethical theory. Firstly, it is very restrictive in its scope, since supporters of natural law claim that only what is natural is good. This leaves little room for man and the world to develop, since over the centuries man has developed in many ways so that what is considered natural in many cases seems outdated or has been superseded in some way. For instance, strict supporters of natural law would argue that fertility treatment was not natural since if someone is not able to have a child naturally then it means that it is God's will for them to remain childless. However, fertility treatment is a blessing for many people who are desperate to have a child and it could be said that it is a way that God has provided for man to discover, which brings happiness to many people. An important argument in favour of this kind of discovery is that if it is there to be discovered, God has put it there for man to investigate and to use for his benefit and so it is not really unnatural.

*This is starting to feel very turgid. An essay that consists of rambling examples or* case studies soon digs itself into the ground since there are only so many marks that can be awarded for this rather general knowledge-type approach.

In the modern world man uses many things that might not be considered natural but which do bring good. For example, many medical treatments and surgical techniques lengthen people's life spans and enable them to live a good quality of life when in previous centuries they would have died. Although it may not be good to keep people alive indefinitely on a life-support machine, surely it is good to be able to transplant organs or bone marrow from willing donors. In theory this is unnatural since it could not happen in the natural world, but it brings happiness to those in great need so it would be difficult to maintain an argument that it was wrong.

e More examples...deadly stuff! Good theoretical knowledge and understanding will always be characterised by strong evaluation rather than this anecdotal style.

Natural law theory could also be said to be very limiting in its idea that everyone has a single purpose. This suggests that we might only have one talent, for example, and that if we do not find it and use it, we have missed out on what God intended for us to do. Also, if man's ultimate purpose is to have a relationship with God then atheists have utterly failed. Does this mean that they can never do what is good? This brings us back to the question of whether goodness and morality can only ever be determined by God.

e This is a potentially interesting link, but the candidate has not developed it into something more substantial.

However, natural law theory is a very simple and direct way of attempting to establish what is good. It is accessible to everyone since it only requires us to look at the natural order and so in theory everyone should be able to subscribe to it.

e This basic conclusion should have examined the strengths of the theory in rather more detail. Overall, a very run-of-the-mill answer that would not earn above a C grade.

# Abortion

'Every pregnant woman has the absolute right to choose to have an abortion.'
Discuss.

(20 marks)

## A-grade answer to A2 question 7

The particular issue addressed in this question is one at the heart of the abortion
dilemma: whose decision should be allowed to predominate when deciding whether
a woman should have an abortion? There are many parties who could claim to be
intimately involved in the decision and to have their rights recognised: the mother,
certainly, but also the father, the law, the medical profession, the church, and those who
represent the interests of the unborn fetus. However, the claim made in the title
challenges rival claims that may be made by any of these other groups to have the right
to be involved in the woman's decision to have an abortion. Our task is to consider
whether anyone else has a right to be involved in the decision and, furthermore,
whether the mother does in any or all circumstances have 'an absolute right to choose
to have an abortion'.

🅔 The key to this question is answering the question set and not running away with
a general waffly answer offering general knowledge on abortion. This candidate
has refreshingly *not* started off with a definition of abortion or with a list of the
conditions necessary for a legal abortion, so there are some early indications that
the question will be answered relevantly and well.

The rights of the mother are undoubtedly very important in the abortion dilemma.
During pregnancy a woman performs a function that only she can perform: to provide
the appropriate and natural conditions in which the child can form, develop and be
born. She is a host to the fetus, whose survival depends on her continued willingness
to be a host. The fetus cannot survive outside the mother's womb until it is viable —
a stage that may be reached as early as 21 weeks, although the baby is then still
dependent upon the care of others. The fetus's survival is not just dependent upon the
mother's psychological willingness to act as host, but on the fitness of the natural
conditions. A natural abortion, or miscarriage, will take place if the environment cannot
support the fetus; clearly this poses no ethical problems. Therapeutic abortion, however,
does have its own characteristic problems, for it implies that the mother is no longer
willing to play host to the fetus. How far does she have an absolute right to declare
herself unwilling?

🅔 The answer is living up to its early promise; the candidate is sticking firmly to the
issue of the mother's rights.

If the mother's life is considered to be of greater value than that of the fetus, then clearly she must have quite considerable rights. She already has an independent life, relationships, and a unique role in the world. Her life could therefore be said to have a greater right of protection than that of the fetus, which as yet has no independent existence and no dependants. The woman may exercise her right to life for many reasons. Her physical life may be in danger unless the pregnancy is terminated; her death would have long-term effects on her existing family, quite apart from her own right to exercise her strong natural impulse to survive. In such a case, the fetus is an unfriendly parasite, and while some women would be prepared to jeopardise their lives to save the fetus, many others would not. The doctrine of double effect could come into play here, allowing even opponents of abortion to grant the woman the right to save her own life, even if the death of the fetus was a secondary effect.

🄴 No case studies! The candidate has covered the concept of double effect without tediously ploughing through different circumstances in which this may apply.

In other cases, however, a woman might want to exercise her right to withdraw from being a host to the fetus for different reasons. Her career or her education might be in jeopardy, or she might not be financially able to support a child. These reasons may be overwhelmingly important to her, but they could be thought to have less moral weight. While her right to life is, arguably, absolute, her right to live her life as she chooses, arguably, is not.

It is in this case that those who represent the rights of the fetus might argue that the child's rights are absolute. The fetus too has a right to life that might be thought to outweigh any right that the mother has. Even if the mother does not feel able to care and provide for the child after birth, defenders of the fetus's rights might claim that she does not thereby have the right to deprive it of life. Once conception has taken place, the fetus has a right to life that must be honoured and the mother must accept responsibility for its life until such time as care can be handed over to foster or adoptive parents.

🄴 The candidate has moved on to consider the rights of the fetus while still keeping the issue of the conflicting rights of the mother firmly in focus.

The defenders of the rights of the fetus might maintain that its rights are no less even if it seems likely that the baby will be born handicapped or suffering from a congenital sickness. It is often claimed that it is in the best interests of the fetus not to allow it to come to full term if it is then to be destined to live a life of pain, but defenders of the fetus's rights can counterclaim that we have no authority to make that decision or to make judgements about perceived quality of life. In many cases, a child born with every conceivable advantage might suffer greatly in later life, so it is impossible to make an *a priori* judgement.

For religious believers, the rights of the mother should not violate the principle of the sanctity of life. This is based on the teaching of Genesis 2:7: 'Then the Lord God formed man of dust from the ground, and breathed into his nostrils the breath of life, and man became a living being.' Psalm 139:13f. also supports the view that God is responsible for the existence of all human life: 'For thou didst form my inward parts, thou didst knit me together in my mother's womb. I praise thee, for I am fearfully and wonderfully made.' The prophet Jeremiah was told by God: 'Before I formed you in the womb I knew you, and before you were born I consecrated you' (Jeremiah 1:5). The New Testament continues to support the principle. For example, in Acts 17:25 Paul declares: 'He himself gives to all men life and breath and everything.' A strictly biblical approach to abortion will therefore deny an absolute right to the mother if the sanctity or sacredness of life is ignored in allowing her to exercise such a right.

> Biblical material, well learned and relevantly applied, is used to support the philosophical principles outlined in the essay, not in place of them.

In support of the mother's absolute rights, Judith Thomson argued the case of the famous violinist in *A Defence of Abortion* (1971). If a woman were to wake to find that a famous violinist whose kidneys had failed had been plugged into her blood supply and would continue to be attached to her in this way for 9 months, she would be under no moral obligation to agree to continue the procedure. If she did agree, it would not be out of moral compulsion, but out of compassion. Thompson argued that pregnancy is an analogous situation, and the woman should be able to choose whether or not to carry the child to full term without the moral obligation to do so. The only provisos she made were that the woman should have taken reasonable precautions to prevent it happening, and if continuing the pregnancy meant only a minor inconvenience to her, then she should do so.

> A classic critique which is never out of place in an essay on this topic.

Finally, what right does the state have in these matters? Prior to 1967, abortion was technically illegal, and, in the interests of protecting the life of the mother from the effects of an illegal abortion, the Abortion Act allowed for legal abortions under strictly controlled conditions. The Act does not permit abortion on demand; two doctors must agree to the termination, and any medical practitioner has the right to refuse to make a recommendation. Nevertheless, pro-life supporters claim that the Act has effectively legalised the murder of thousands of fetuses every year, protecting the absolute rights of the mother over those of the fetus.

> This well-balanced and carefully crafted essay thoroughly deserves an A grade.

■ ■ ■

## C-grade answer to A2 question 7

Abortion is the premature termination of the life of the fetus before it comes to full term. A woman may seek an abortion for a variety of reasons: if her life or health is in jeopardy; if the health or well-being of existing children is threatened; if the fetus is

likely to be born seriously handicapped; or if her psychological health is likely to be undermined. Under the Abortion Act two doctors need to agree to a woman having an abortion, and it must take place by 24 weeks into the pregnancy. Only if the woman's life is seriously in danger could she have an abortion after this date. An abortion may be performed in a number of ways, most usually by a D and C, or by vacuum extraction of the fetus. Most abortions take place for therapeutic reasons, because the mother is unable to cope psychologically with having a baby, although this may be because it would interfere with her career or education, for example.

> **e** This is a rather depressing start. The candidate seems determined to get in as many facts about abortion as possible in the first paragraph, without giving much indication that the question is actually going to be addressed.

There are many reasons why people are both for and against abortion. The main reason why some people argue that the mother has a right to have an abortion is because she should be allowed to have freedom of choice. It is her body and it is she who will have to carry the child for 9 months, even if she then chooses to hand the baby over for adoption. Judith Thompson uses the analogy of the famous violinist and compares the pregnant woman with a woman who has been attached to a violinist for 9 months, giving them life support. He will die if she refuses to remain attached to him, but Thompson makes the point that she is entitled to refuse since the violinist is a parasite. The fetus is a parasite in the same way, she suggests, and the mother should not be obliged to continue the pregnancy.

> **e** This well-known example is used appropriately here. Hopefully, the candidate will go on to develop a clear line of argument concerning the mother's rights versus the rights of others.

Other reasons given against abortion concern the life of the fetus. Religious believers usually agree that life is sacred, and it should be protected, not destroyed. If this is the case, then to destroy a fetus through abortion goes against the principle of the sanctity of life. Most religious believers, especially Evangelicals and Roman Catholics, will say that abortion is always wrong in any situation. The only way to get round this is the doctrine of double effect. If the woman needs a life-saving operation, which will terminate the pregnancy, then the primary aim is to save the mother's life rather than abort the baby and this is acceptable. However, if the woman wanted an abortion just so she could go on holiday or accept a new job, the principle would not work.

> **e** In general terms, the candidate is discussing the mother's rights, but this still has the feel of a rather random attack: some shots are hitting the target but rather more by luck than judgement. It is a pity that the concept of the sanctity of life has not been developed more fully with regard to, say, the fetus's right to life.

Other reasons against abortion include the fact that it removes any choice from the fetus in the future. Even if we know that a child may be born with disabilities or an illness that may lead to an early death, it is not up to others to make the decision that it would be better for them not to be born. We cannot know all the consequences of any event which lies in the future, and to make a decision that a child would be better off not born completely eliminates the possibility that he or she will bring happiness to others, and may have a successful life.

Even if the mother does not want to keep the baby, there are many people who want to adopt and there is no reason why she should be forced to look after the baby once it is born since there are far fewer babies available for adoption than there are couples who want to adopt. In some cases, the mother may even decide she wants to keep the baby herself and would have deeply regretted having an abortion. Abortion is thought to be one of the most stressful experiences that a woman can go through and many suffer psychologically afterwards.

ℯ This is all basically relevant material, but it lacks the intellectual rigour of the A-grade essay.

Finally, if the fetus is a person then there are great difficulties saying that it can be aborted. If the killing of a person is murder, then arguably abortion is murder if the fetus is more than just a potential person, or a clump of cells, or part of the mother's body with no separate identity. Aquinas argued that ensoulment was a key stage in defining the fetus as a person — 40 days for males and 90 days for females. Although this is an outdated way of looking at it, there are still stages that may be considered to be important in the development of the fetus after which no abortion could be considered. These may range from conception to viability, depending on how strict a view people might take.

ℯ This is potentially interesting and could have been incorporated into the essay rather more productively had it been introduced and developed earlier on.

Whether the mother has an absolute right to abortion will therefore depend on whether her rights are considered to be more important than the rights of the fetus. If it is thought that the fetus should have its rights fully recognised even though they are potential and not actual, then her rights cannot be absolute.

ℯ The candidate has missed the opportunity to consider the rights of others — father, doctors, the church, other relatives perhaps. This simple approach to the question, whilst not inaccurate, could have been much more fully substantiated. It would yield a C grade.

# Synoptic question

The new specifications for all boards require candidates to complete a synoptic unit either as coursework or under exam conditions. The principle behind this is that students of religious studies should be able to identify and critically evaluate the links between different parts of their specification. The potential range of combinations is enormous: philosophy of religion and world religions; philosophy and ethics; philosophy and Old Testament/Jewish Bible; philosophy and New Testament; philosophy and church history. The last essay in this book is a sample synoptic question — with just one A-grade answer — on a popular combination, philosophy of religion and New Testament. Even if this is not the particular combination that you will be taking, read it carefully and take note of the comments made about its features. It is written as if under exam conditions and hence it is not a piece of coursework that would be subject to certain scholarly conventions such as footnoting.

Synoptic questions demand that you are able to examine a topic — in this case, miracles — from the perspective of two disciplines within your subject. This question demands that the candidate demonstrates knowledge of biblical material and its interpretation, along with philosophical definition of miracles and issues about the nature of God and his action in the world. Too much emphasis on either the New Testament or philosophy will unbalance the essay. It is up to you to work on identifying the links between the approaches and to think laterally about the topic under discussion.

If you are completing a synoptic question under timed exam conditions, you must practise before the examination. Although the titles will vary from year to year, the principles of the question and the links between the disciplines remain the same. You should therefore not have any nasty surprises if you have prepared diligently.

# Philosophy and New Testament

'The accounts of miracle stories in the New Testament support a belief in a God who can perform logically impossible actions.' Discuss.     (50 marks)

### A-grade answer to A2 question 8

The logically impossible is something that is not only outside our experience, but which logic, reason and the nature of the universe tell us cannot occur. It defies logic that the Red Sea should part, that the sun should reverse its course, or that the dead should be raised. We know that water does not turn into wine, that missing limbs do not regrow, and that the paralysed might conceivably walk again only if they have undergone long, expensive and intensive therapy. Nevertheless, not only the Bible but also a wealth of Christian testimony handed down over the centuries and in the present day suggest otherwise. Bible-believing Christians, and those who have experienced miracles in their lives and in the lives of others, claim not only that God does perform miracles but also that the kind of miracle described above is not even logically impossible. It may be an infrequent occurrence, but not logically impossible.

The introduction has immediately made connections between both disciplines with some consideration of the phrase 'logically impossible' (philosophy) and the kind of biblical miracles that may be considered useful in answering this question (New Testament).

Strictly speaking, therefore, the logically impossible is that which is not merely unexpected or unusual, but that which is inconceivable. It is inconceivable that God could make a square circle, for this would defy the boundaries of logic and reasoning. It is inconceivable that God should commit suicide, or even, perhaps, that he could make a stone too heavy for him to lift (should God engage in such activities). But it is not inconceivable that God should raise the dead, for the whole world order as we know it would not fall apart if he did. While experience tells us that the dead, once dead, remain so, is it actually logically impossible that the dead should rise? Is it utterly inconceivable that a blind man see again, or even for the first time, or that a woman who has suffered years of chronic back pain be instantly cured?

The candidate is leaving us in no doubt that he or she has understood that a consideration of what would constitute the 'logically impossible' is essential for this answer. A good philosophical awareness is demonstrated in so doing.

The New Testament is full of such accounts. Although miracles are clearly not presented as the reason why men and women should put their faith in Jesus, they were an intrinsic part of his ministry. Miracles confirmed belief — 'This, the first of his signs, Jesus did at Cana in Galilee, and manifested his glory, and his disciples believed in him' (John 2:11); they demonstrated Jesus's authority — 'What is this? With authority he commands even the unclean spirits and they obey him' (Mark 1:27); and they identified him as the Son of God — 'And when they got into the boat, the wind ceased, and those in the boat worshipped him, saying, "Truly you are the Son of God"' (Matthew 14:32–33). Such events were greeted with amazement, wonder and awe; they were evidently beyond the experience of those who witnessed them, who demanded an explanation for them or who were further convinced of what they had already believed about Jesus as a result of listening to his teaching. Jesus performed deeds through the divine power working in him which were at least beyond regular experience, and at most were violations of a natural law: 'transgressions of a law of nature, by the volition of the deity, or by the interposition of some invisible agent' (David Hume's classic definition of miracle).

 Now the candidate has demonstrated excellent biblical textual knowledge, while still concluding the paragraph with a definition of miracle from an important philosopher.

Aquinas proposed three categories of miracle: first, those acts done by God that nature cannot do. When Jesus raised Lazarus, Jairus's daughter, or the widow of Nain's son, or when Paul brought the unfortunate Eutychus back to life, they were surely doing that which nature cannot do. If these characters were actually dead, then we know that since death is an irreversible state, they could not have been restored to life without the direct power and agency of God. Aquinas's second category of miracles is of things 'done by God that nature could do, but not in this order'. Such miracles might include the healing of the paralysed man. Indeed, many of Jesus's miracles fall into this category: acts that we could conceive of happening within the course of nature, but which experience generally tells us do not occur. However, they are not logically impossible. Where all treatments have failed and the cancer patient is sent home to accept an inevitable death sentence, no one might expect their recovery. But there would be no breach of natural law or logical impossibility if they nevertheless, unexpectedly, and contrary to previous experience drawn from similar cases, went into remission. In such cases, although we might claim that there was no obvious explanation for the recovery, we might equally claim that the simplest explanation was that God intervened miraculously. The official's son (John 4:46–54), the woman who had suffered 12 years of internal bleeding (Luke 8:43–48 &//s) and the leper (Matthew 8:1–4 &//s) enjoyed such healings, which were not logically impossible but were certainly beyond what they expected of nature.

The third category of miracles that Aquinas considered were those things done by God that nature could do, but without the workings of nature. When Jesus cured Peter's mother-in-law of a fever (Mark 1:29–31) there was no suggestion that she was on her deathbed. She presumably had been suffering from something akin to a severe cold, or flu or the like, and would have recovered naturally in due course, but Jesus's action expedited the process. Many Christians may believe that God regularly answers their prayers in such a way, so that they may indeed not even consider such events especially miraculous (in the strongest sense of the term), but rather loving responses by God to the prayers of his people.

 An excellent example of good synoptic practice here, interweaving philosophy (Aquinas's definitions) with New Testament material.

In the New Testament, therefore, Jesus and others (Paul, Peter and John, the 72 sent out by Jesus) perform miracles that fall into all these categories — not only the logically impossible, but events that may warrant the designation miracle but that involve no direct breach of natural law, or violation of logic and reason.

 Having established a very clear line of argument about the nature of miracle in the New Testament and philosophical definitions of miracles, the candidate now begins the all-important evaluation.

However, it is important to consider the reliability of the New Testament accounts before we conclude that they accurately relate instances of the logically impossible. If, for our purposes, we define a logically impossible event as one that violates a law of nature, we must consider whether the law of nature actually has been broken, whether there was a law of nature at work in the first place (in order for it to be broken), and whether the incident has been correctly understood by those who witnessed it or recorded it.

> As in all good exam essays, use of scholarship should be discerning and relevant. In a synoptic essay that is — in theory — twice as long as a regular exam essay, the student should perhaps be looking to include five or six scholarly views, definitions or quotations.

R. H. Fuller argued that we should be wary of claiming that the New Testament miracles are violations of a natural law, since the biblical writers had no concept of natural law as we have today. To them, events were unusual, significant or important, but the evangelists themselves made no *claims* that Jesus broke natural laws. They did claim that his actions were sufficiently significant to lead observers to evaluate him as possessing divine power, even to be equal to God, but claims that natural laws were violated are left to later interpreters to make.

> Here and in the next paragraph the philosophical and biblical material continues to be impressively interwoven, demonstrating that the candidate has an understanding of both, and of the all-important connections between them.

Furthermore, what we may read at one level as biblical accounts of violations of natural law may be explained quite easily in other ways. Rudolph Bultmann famously wrote: 'It is impossible to use electric light and the wireless and to avail ourselves of modern medical and surgical discoveries and, at the same time, to believe in the New Testament world of demons and spirits.' In other words, biblical accounts of miracles owe their origin to an age when the world-view was significantly different from that of our own scientific, rational age. The biblical writers may well have interpreted recovery of the Gerasene Demoniac to the casting out of demons, but modern psychiatry might identify him as a victim of multiple personality disorder, calmed and soothed by the presence of Jesus. In a sense, we no longer need (although we may choose) to explain phenomena in terms of the spirit world, and this gives rise to the question of whether the biblical writers were accurate in their assessment of events. Did the Red Sea part through a miraculous act of God, or did a freak wind blow back the waters at the precise moment that the Israelites were pondering how to circumnavigate this watery obstacle, an event so fortuitous and 'stupendous as to be ever impressed on her memory' (John Bright)?

> This paragraph offers more evaluation from both perspectives.

Such interpretations do not necessarily eliminate God from the equation, but they force us to reconsider our understanding of what occurred. God's hand, or that of Jesus, may

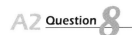 

still be at work in an event that goes utterly against our expectations and that blesses the recipient in ways that had seemed otherwise impossible, but this need not demand that the natural law be broken or that logical impossibilities are achieved. God may work within rather than outside the natural order, bringing to pass things that may happen naturally, but at such times and places when he can breach the epistemic distance and make himself and his nature directly evident to his people. Richard Swinburne suggested: 'If there is a God, one might well expect him to make his presence known to men, not merely through the overall pattern of the universe in which he placed them, but by dealing more intimately and personally with them.' It is not necessary that God do the logically impossible in order to interact with his people in this way, although if he is omnipotent there are strong reasons for believers to maintain that sometimes he will do so.

If the New Testament does support a belief that God can do the logically impossible, there must still be good reasons for him to do so, and a God who acts arbitrarily, or appears to violate the natural order of things without there being obvious benefits for his people, is not a God worthy of worship. If squaring the circle or creating a married bachelor is a truly logically impossible act, then can God perform such a deed? More to the point, should he? If God is omnipotent then presumably he can; if God creates the laws of nature they are within his control, and so too are the laws of logic, mathematics and analytic reasoning. He could change them at will, and declare the triangle a circle, or the queen a king. However, what purpose would be achieved by his so doing? The New Testament does not support such a portrait of God, since all the miracles performed by Jesus or the apostles have a clear purpose: to demonstrate the glory of God. God's glory would not be enhanced by geometric tricks or language games like those of the logical positivists! Not surprisingly, therefore, the New Testament writers, while supporting (within their understanding of such phenomena) a God who may bring men and women back from the dead, and calm the sea with an authoritative word, do not propose a God who arbitrarily changes the principles and laws which hold the universe in place.

The essay concludes with a paragraph that is characterised — as the whole piece has been — with a smooth interweaving of philosophical evaluation and biblical knowledge. This is a very high-level answer indeed.